# Saint Petersburg
## Museums, Palaces, and Historic Collections

CATHY GIANGRANDE

with an introduction by
JOHN JULIUS NORWICH

D0914602

BUNKER HILL PUBLISHING
BOSTON • LONDON

# *For Paul, Chris and Alex*

First published in 2003 by Bunker Hill Publishing Inc.
26 Adams Street, Charlestown, MA 02129 USA
6 The Colonnade, Rye Road, Hawkhurst, Kent TN18 4ES UK

10 9 8 7 6 5 4 3 2 1

Copyright © Cathy Giangrande
All rights reserved

Library of Congress Cataloging in Publication Data available from the publisher's office

ISBN 1 59373 000 4

Designed by Louise Millar

Printed in China by Jade Productions

The publishers wish to thank the CSB Group of companies, CSB Ltd, CSB Financial Systems Ltd,
Total Objects Ltd, and CSBIEE for their generous support of this publication. In particular their Chairman
Larry Sullivan and Vladimir Serbin, General Director of CSBIEE, who have both fostered their organisations'
commercial and community interests in St. Petersburg. These interests include the introduction
of established business networks that initiate solid commercial partnerships and ongoing support
of local orphanages by the group of companies and their associates.
For further information see: www.coins-global.com, www.oasissolutions.co.uk, www.totalobjects.co.uk, www.csbi.ru

The author would also like to thank Sergei E. Korneiev, Vice-President
of the Russian Union of Travel Industry, for his support.

# Contents

# Author's Note

Founded by Peter the Great in 1703, St Petersburg was for Russia, "a window to the west". Three hundred years later, the city known as the "Venice of the North" is one of the world's great cultural hubs and the artistic heart of European Russia. Brimming with over 260 museums, thousands of monuments and breathtaking palaces everywhere you look, it's fitting that over a decade ago UNESCO inscribed St Petersburg and its suburban palaces and parks on the World Heritage List. This guide however, does not include an entry on the Hermitage or the State Russian Museum, as these well-known collections can be found in any book on the city. Instead, you will discover a selection highlighting over 50 of the more exotic, lesser-known and in some cases, recently opened sites, from the museums on bread, circus art and vodka, to the palaces at Oranienbaum on the Gulf of Finland as well as the string of memorial apartment museums that mark the rich mix of writers, musicians and artists that St Petersburg has been home to.

To assist the user of this guide, the sites have been placed into seven chapters according to their locations. The center of the city has been divided into six manageable chunks as defined by the borders of the river Neva that snakes through the city and the circles of canals, with an additional seventh one for the sites in the suburbs. These areas are defined by the colored symbols on the endpaper maps, each numbered to pinpoint the museums and palaces within, allowing you to plan your daily route. As well as using these maps, you may also like to purchase a detailed city map. It is advisable to call before visiting, as many have a habit of closing on a whim. If you are dialling from abroad or outside the city centre you must also dial 812, the area code for St Petersburg. It is standard practice at most museums to charge higher entrance fees for foreigners and many also charge if you wish to take photographs. Each entry lists the name of the site in both English and Russian, and includes the transliteration based on the system created by the United States Library of Congress, which uses 'i' instead of 'y'.

It's appropriate, that in the year celebrating the tercentenary of the city, this guide has been produced to aid those flocking to join in the festivities and enjoy it magnificence. It's a guide that will enable even the less intrepid visitor to reach the beating heart of this culturally rich city.

CATHY GIANGRANDE

# Introduction

St. Petersburg is, as we all agree, one of the most beautiful cities of Europe; but because of its checkered twentieth-century history, it is still one of the least known. We may be on easy familiar terms with Paris and Rome and Madrid, but for most of us St. Petersburg is no more than an acquaintance—and for a good many of us not even that. We are still getting to know it, and for such a purpose we need all the help we can lay our hands on.

The one building that we all know, if we have ever set foot in the city, is the Hermitage. Its immensity, its superb situation looking over the Neva, its exuberant exterior color scheme—a dazzling green and white—and its unbelievably sumptuous interiors, to say nothing of the fabulous wealth of its collections, all combine to make it a world-class phenomenon, still unforgettable after the most fleeting visit. It tends, however, to be hideously crowded and, by virtue of its size alone, cannot fail to be both physically and mentally exhausting. But take comfort: the Hermitage is by no means the only museum in St. Petersburg. There are scores of others, large and small—some in palaces, many more in unassuming little buildings which you could easily walk straight past without noticing. In very few will you have any trouble with crowds, and from most of them you will not only enjoy yourself but will emerge at the end as fresh as a daisy. On the other hand, they have not been invariably easy to learn about by any means, still less to find.

Until now. You now hold in your hands the first guidebook exclusively devoted to the lesser-known museums of the city. It will tell you what they are, where they are, when they are open, and what you can expect to find in them. It will open up a new world, a St. Petersburg that lies behind the great palaces and churches; that has seen much, experienced much, and suffered much; and that is prepared to reveal its secrets to anyone who takes the trouble to investigate and inquire. This book will make it immeasurably easier for you to do so.

JOHN JULIUS NORWICH

# Museum on the Cruiser *Avrora*
Музей на крейсере "Аврора"
## Muzei na kreisere "Avrora"

1

**Address:** Kreiser "Aurora," Petrovskaia
Naberezhnaia, St. Petersburg 197046
**Tel:** 230-8440
**Website:** www.aurora.org.ru

**Open:** 10:30 A.M.–4 P.M.; closed Mondays and
and Fridays
**Metro:** Gor'kovskaia
**Kiosk/shop**

Anchored in the river Neva, close to the Nakhimov Naval School, stands the ironclad cruiser *Avrora*, the barrel of its 155mm bow gun pointing toward the opposite bank. This is the warship that signaled the start of the October Revolution on October 25 1917. At 9:40 P.M. that evening, with searchlights pointed at the Winter Palace, Lenin ordered a blank shot to be fired from its bow to signal the storming of the palace. Today, the *Avrora* stands as a symbol of revolutionary Russia, as well as a monument saluting the skills of Russian shipbuilding.

Designed by K. K. Ratnik, business manager of the Baltiiskii Ironworks and built at the New Admiralty yards in 1897–1900, the cruiser was equipped with the latest armaments, including 75mm Cane guns, 37mm Gochkis guns, and submersible torpedo tubes. Dispatched to the Far East in 1903, but soon withdrawn because of the start of the Russo-Japanese War, she did not see fire until 1904–05 in the Pacific, when she took part in the Tsushima battle against the Japanese fleet.

Subsequently, the *Avrora* became a training ship for cadets and reefers of the Marine Cadet Corps until the First World War, when she engaged in service once again and was overhauled with new, more powerful weapons and a radio station. Following the firing of its historic shot in 1917, sailors on the vessel fought in the Russian Civil War of 1918–20 and during the Second World War the ship's crew participated in the defense of Leningrad. Damaged by German artillery in 1941, when she was anchored in the vicinity of Oranienbaum, near Leningrad, she flooded, but was raised before the end of the war in

1944, when it was decided the cruiser would become a memorial to the Revolution.

*Below decks on the* Avrora

Both the exterior and most of the inner rooms were restored, and pieces that were badly damaged, like the funnels, were replaced. The ship became a training base for pupils from the Nakhimov Naval School, who maintained her until 1956, when the cruiser became a museum. Today, six halls on the gun deck exhibit over 1,000 paintings, banners, documents, personal photos, orders, and medals of those who served on the vessel, documenting the cruiser's history. There are models of both old and new Russian warships and displays of gifts presented by foreign governments and military organizations. Besides these exhibits, there are tours of the engine and boiler rooms and an artillery tour that takes you through the upper deck, conning tower, and radio station, where you can see the devices and equipment used at beginning of the 20th century.

7

# Komarov Botanical Museum and Gardens
Ботанический музей им. В.Л. Комарова
**Botanicheskii muzei im. V. L. Komarova**

---

**Address:** 2 Ulitsa Professora Popova,
   St. Petersburg 197376
**Tel:** 234-8439 / 234-0673 / 234-8470
**Website:** www.museum.ru/M100
**E-mail:** m100@mail.museum.ru
**Open:** 10 A.M. –6 P.M. daily, May 15–September 30
**Directions:** Bus 46 runs from the metro to the
   museum

Excursions to the various greenhouses are available for visitors depending on the time: (1) "Tropical plants"—all year round; (2) "Subtropical plants"—from September 15 to June 1; (3) "Aquatic plants"—from the May 15 to September 30 (4) "Christmas and New Year plants"—during December

---

While Peter the Great was busy learning about shipbuilding and establishing the Imperial Navy, he sent his lieutenants to comb the world in search of natural and artificial curiosities to fill his *Kunstkammer*. Among these were numerous plant specimens. However, his interest extended beyond just collecting—he also understood the benefits of medicinal herbs, and in 1714 ordered that an apothecary garden be constructed on Aptekarskii Island, on the Petrograd side of St. Petersburg. It supplied St. Petersburg's apothecaries with herbal plants, and in 1720 the first greenhouse was built so that plants could be grown year-round. It became the richest collection of medicinal plants in Europe and by 1823 was known as the Imperial Botanical Gardens.

   The collection expanded quickly with specimens gathered from extensive explo-

rations of flora in Russia and foreign countries, including an outstation in Rio de Janeiro. By 1825, under the guidance of the garden's director, F. B. Fisher, it had grown to include 25 greenhouses. During the late 19th and early 20th centuries, large herbarium collections were acquired following expeditions undertaken by the Colonial Department of the Russian Ministry of Agriculture led by famous botanists, including K. I. Maximowicz, V. L. Komarov (after whom the museum is named), and P. N. Krilov. Prior to the Revolution these gardens rivaled their nearest competitor, London's Kew Gardens. Bombing during the wars destroyed many of the greenhouses, leaving the gardens in ruin, but gradually many were restored and in place of one of the greenhouses the Botanical Museum was built. Bullet holes can still be seen in the wrought

*The Medicinal Orangery built in 1888-9*

iron of the Palm Orangery. However, despite the ravages of war, there are 26 working hothouses/orangeries on the grounds of the gardens.

Today, the garden contains an enormous collection of trees and shrubs from all over Russia, North America, Europe, Japan, and China. The Institute's collection contains the world's second largest herbarium, which is particularly rich in type specimens. About half of the type specimens of the world's collections of perennial *Triticeae* grasses may be found here, and for botanists working on plant taxonomy, the Institute's Siberia and Far East Herbarium is one of the most important in the world. The library contains volumes of original botanical watercolors, including those purchased by Peter the Great from the Dutch botanist Maria Sybilla Merian. Arranged within the museum are themed displays, such as the evolution of plants, supplemented by specimens from the Botanical Gardens.

*The herbarium of ENS Abraham*

**9**

# Historical Artillery Museum
Военно-исторический музей артилерии
## Voenno-istoricheskii muzei artilerii

**3**

**Address:** 7 Aleksandrovskii Park,
St. Petersburg 197049
**Tel:** 238-4704 / 232-4739 / 233-4697 /
232-0296

**Website:** www.museum.ru/M152
**Open:** 11 A.M. –6 P.M. Wednesday to Sunday
closed the last Thursday of every month
**Metro:** Gor'kovskaia

Across the Kronverk Ditch from the Peter and Paul Fortress Golovkin Bastion stands a vast horseshoe-shaped arsenal, fronted by tanks and missile launchers. Inside, the Artillery Museum, founded in 1703, celebrates what the Russian military calls the "Queen of Arms." The Crownwork Arsenal, built between 1849 and 1860 and designed by the architect Peter Tamanskii, became home to this collection in 1868. It was not until almost a century later that it took on its present name after merging its collections with those of the Central Historical Museum of Military Engineering in Moscow.

The collection is pure delight to those fond of military weapons, uniforms, and the paraphernalia of war. Besides the vast display of artillery, signal equipment, and military vehicles on show in the courtyard outside, there are 14 halls (two used for special exhibitions) crammed full of arms and armor reflecting Russian military history. From medieval times there is the first Russian harquebus and an early bronze gun cast in Iakov in 1491. Other halls feature a bronze mortar dating

*General Suvorov's coach used at the Battle of Borodino*

from the early 17th century, the pike that Peter the Great carried as a foot soldier, an ornate coach from which General Suvorov harangued his troops at the Battle of Borodino, and a massive display of regimental banners, medals, and orders, all originating from the Military Hall (which later moved here) of the arsenal on Liteinii Prospect.

Additional highlights include Lenin's armored car, *Enemy of Capital,* on which he rode in triumph from Finland Station on April 3, 1917, making speeches from its gun turret. There is also an array of snazzy Red Army uniforms designed by a Futurist artist later killed in the purges. Among the Second World War exhibits are the Katiusha multiple-rocket launcher, a huge mural of trench warfare at Stalingrad, and a diorama of Kursk, where the biggest tank battle in history took place. There is a section dedicated to "Signals," culminating in a model of the ruined Reichstag and a painting of Hitler committing suicide.

*Rocket engines*

*Bronze mortar chosen by Peter the Great for the "Preservation of Eternal Glory"*

Scattered throughout the exhibits are a few uniforms and portraits of famous Russian generals, including Prince Grigorii Potemkin (1739–91), who served during Catherine the Great's reign, and Barclay de Tolly (1761–1818), of Scottish descent, who served under Potemkin and later won the title of Prince of the Russian Empire under Tsar Aleksandr I. There is also a special exhibit of garments devoted to the military uniforms and uniformed portraits of Russian tsars and their families from Peter I to Nicholas II.

A lecture hall and cinema have daily shows —for times and details, check with the museum when you arrive.

**11**

# Peter and Paul Fortress Петропавловская крепость Petropavlovskaia krepost

## A Branch of the State History Museum
### *including the following:*

**St. Peter and Paul's Cathedral** Петропавловский собор **Petropavlovskii sobor**
**Engineers' House** Инженерный дом **Inzhenernii dom**
**Prison Museum** Тюрьемный музей **Tiur' emnii muzei**
**Printing Workshop** Печатня **Pechatnia**
**Boathouse** Ботный дом **Botnii dom**
**Commandant's House** Комендантский дом **Komendantskii dom**
**Museum of Cosmonautics and Rocket Technology** Музей космонавтики и ракетной техники **Muzei kosmonavtiki i raketnoi tekhniki**
**Mint Works** Монетный двор **Monetnii dvor**

**Address :** 3 Petropavlovskaia Krepost',
St. Petersburg 197046
**Tel:** 238-4540 / 238-4511
**Website:** www.museum.ru/museum/gmispb
**Open:** daily 11 A.M.–6 P.M. daily, except Tuesdays (11 A.M.–4 P.M.; closed Wednesdays and the last Tuesday of every month.

**Metro:** Gor'kovskaia
**Kiosk/shop, lecture/cinema hall, café/bar**
It's worth asking about tours—a recent addition is the "Neva Panorama" tour, which takes visitors along wooden platforms attached to a section of the upper part of the ramparts and several of the bastions.

*The spire of the St. Peter and Paul Cathedral*

*Aerial view of the Peter and Paul Fortress*

When Peter rode with his horsemen toward the barren marshlands surrounding the River Neva in the spring of 1703, he was looking for a place to build a fort to protect these newly acquired lands from their former owners, the Swedish. One story recounts Peter jumping down from his horse and using his bayonet to cut two strips of turf from the center of Zaiachii Island (Hare's Island). Laying them across each other to form a cross, he boldly announced that a church in the names of the saints Peter and Paul would be built here.

Several months later the hexagonal Peter and Paul Fortress was well on its way to completion, with the loss of thousands of conscripts working in the most appalling conditions. Within years—and with the loss of even more lives—the surrounding land, on which there were already settlements (as well as residence of Swedish officials), emerged as the resplendent city of St. Petersburg.

The original fortifications, made of earth, were replaced by stone in 1706 after Peter laid the foundation stone of the Menshikov

**13**

*The St. Peter and Paul Cathedral with the Boathouse to the left*

Bastion. The bastions at the six corners are named in honor of Peter and five of his associates who assisted in the construction. Over the following decades, the fortress was the nucleus of the new city, where, inspired by the architecture of western Europe, it became a collection of structures including the Mint, the Commandant's House, St. Peter's Gate, the Boathouse, the Engineers' House, and **St. Peter and Paul's Cathedral**, erected in 1712. A central feature of the fortress, it is crowned with a gilded spire and its bell tower still makes it the city's tallest architectural monument (402 ft/122.5 m). The Baroque style, gilded iconostasis (1722–29) is the central feature of the cathedral, and it famously serves as a mausoleum for the members of the Romanov Dynasty. It contains the tombs of the Romanov emperors, beginning with Peter I (except for Peter II and Ivan VI Antonovich) and many members of the imperial family. To the east of the cathedral is the **Grand Dukes' Burial Vault**, where, because of lack of space in the cathedral, other members of the imperial family are buried. Near the cathedral, in the middle of the fortress, is the controversial statue of Peter by the Russian émigré sculptor Mikhail Shemiakin, erected in 1991. It's a rather unflattering piece showing Peter with long, thin limbs and a rather small head devoid of its wig.

The fortress is well known to all the citizens and tourists, but only a few people know that the central reserve of the **Museum of the History of St. Petersburg**, one of the major

*The cathedral's nave and baroque iconostasis*

*The prison in the Trubetskoi Bastion*

museums of Russia, is situated here. Storage for what now numbers over 1 million art and historical objects connected to the history of the city are located in the old ramparts, with a selection shown in various buildings within the fortress. There are extensive collections of paintings and drawings from the 18th to the beginning of the 20th century, decorative arts, ceramics and glass, postcards and coins. The core of the collection was amassed in 1907 by the architects and artists and was known as the **Museum of Old St. Petersburg**. The **Engineers' House** (built in 1748–49 and formerly the workshops and storerooms of the Engineering Department, which assisted in the construction of the fortress) has since been restored to accommodate many of the prized items from the Museum of the History of St. Petersburg. On display is an array of items, including documents, photographs, banners, and engravings, that tell us about the city's heritage.

The museum's oldest exhibition is located in the former Trubetskoi Bastion, now housing the **Prison Museum**. The museum fails to convey the full horror of the conditions in tsarist times, when prisoners were kept in the casemates of the fortress and later in the "secret house" in the Aleksei Ravelin, a building that no longer survives. The accessible cells are stark and gloomy, but far worse existed within the ramparts, below the level of the river, where the perpetual damp and cold made tuberculosis inevitable. Prisoners were never allowed to see each other and rarely glimpsed their jailers. Some were denied visitors and reading material for decades. The corridors were carpeted to deaden sound, enabling the "specials" to creep up and spy through the door slits without warning. Anyone caught communicating by tapping out messages ("the prisoners' alphabet") risked being confined to an unheated punishment cell, the *kartser*, and fed on bread and water. Once every two weeks, each inmate was escorted to the bathhouse in the courtyard for a solitary scrub and exercise, but the corridor windows were painted over so that no one could see who was exercising.

The most famous prisoners at the fortress were the son of Peter I, Tsarevich Aleksei; the writer and philosopher Aleksandr Radishchev; the writer Fiodor Dostoievskii; the anarchist Mikhail Bakunin; and the revolutionary Nikolai Chernishchevsii. When the new prison building (which became the museum in 1924) was built in 1870, thousands of prisoners

**15**

spent time in the solitary confinement cells. These prisoners included members of the People's Will organization (formed in 1879, they organized the assassination of Aleksandr II) and, later, participants in the anti-Bolshevik uprising in Kronstadt. A monument and quotation from the anarchist Prince Kropotkin (a former prisoner and author of *In Russian and French Prisons*, London, 1887) commemorate the prisoners' sufferings.

The three casemates of the Neva Ramparts, just to the left of the Neva Gate, are home to a museum complex that includes a history exhibition, a gallery displaying graphic works by St. Petersburg artists, and a working print shop, known as the **Printing Workshop** (*Pechatnia*). Here printing equipment, including original presses, is displayed and used for demonstrations of a variety of techniques, including the production of engravings using wood and metal, etchings, and lithographs. It's worth a trip to the basement to see the original foundations of the printing house.

The **Boathouse**, now used as a visitor's center, also houses a copy (the original is in the Central Naval Museum) of Peter's boat, known as the "Grandfather of the Russian Navy." As a child, Peter used it to perfect his sailing skills, and later, on August 30, 1723, to celebrate Nistad Day (a day marking the signing of the Treaty of Nistad), he steered up the Neva between the Russian Navy warships to honor the boat as well as the creation of the navy.

The former **Commandant's House**, designed by D. Trezzini and built in 1743 with the military engineer de Marine, was originally the living quarters of the commandants, who were usually the outstanding military leaders appointed by the emperor. There were a total of 34 commandant's during tsarist times, and many of them are buried at the cemetery near the east façade of the St. Peter and Paul Cathedral. During the 19th century the house was used for interrogations and court procedures. Today it is used for displays on the history and development of the city from its foundation in 1703 to the mid-19th century.

*The Mint Works*

Founded by the order of Peter I in 1724, the original **Mint Works** were in the ramparts between the Catherine and Trubetskoi Bastions. The building we now see was specially constructed later, in 1798. The Mint Works would have produced not only gold, silver, and copper coinage, but also medals by the best medal designers of the day.

Also a part of this fortress complex is the **Museum of Cosmonautics and Rocket Technology**. Since the Cold War the space program in Russia has been hampered by budget cuts, but Russia remains a great space superpower and has the world's most advanced rocket engine technology. Located here, at the eastern end of the Peter and Paul Fortress, is a fortified structure built in the first half of the 18th century. It was here in the late 1920s that the first Soviet organization engaged in the development of rocket engines and rocket technology had its workshops, experimental laboratories, and design offices. It was known as the Gas-Dynamic Laboratory, or GDL. In line with the Soviet effort to modernize the newly formed Red Army, the engineer I. Tikhomirov was assigned the job of developing "rocket-propelled mines." With a team of ten that later grew to several hundred, they worked here on perfecting military missiles and developing new solid rocket fuel. Nine types of ground, air, and sea-based rockets were tested on the ground. By the late 1920s a separate department of the GDL was devoted to chemical and electrical rocket engine research, under the direction of Valentin Glushko (1908–89), the country's greatest rocket engine designer.

In 1973 the restored designers' rooms, lab workshops, and the high-voltage testing area were opened as a museum that not only traces the roles of the GDL in rocket and space research, but also contains displays devoted to the history of cosmonautics, focusing on the

*Display of cosmonautic equipment*

founders and the pioneering cosmonauts of Soviet space exploration. They include Sergei Korolev (1906–66), the inspirational leader of the space program who co-founded the Moscow rocketry group (and who under Stalin was imprisoned along with V. Glushko; Konstantin E. Tsiolkovskii (1857–1935), who as a mathematician laid out many of the principles of modern space flight; and Nikolai Rukavishnikov (1932–2002), who is well known for one of the most traumatic spacecraft re-entries ever undertaken aboard *Soyuz 33* (one of his spacesuits is on display). Models of various rocket engines, the starting control apparatus of the spaceship *Soyuz 16*, spacesuits, photographs taken by Soviet cosmonauts of the moon and other planets, along with documents complement displays that tell the story of this crucial point in the history of Soviet policy and development of rocket technology. **17**

# Peter the Great's Log Cabin
## Домик Петра Великого
### Domik Petra Velikogo

**5**

**Address:** 6 Petrovskaia Naberezhnaia,
  St. Petersburg 197046
**Tel:** 232-4556 / 232-4576

**Website:** www.museum.ru/M161
**Open:** 10 A.M.–5 P.M., Wednesday to Sunday
**Metro:** Gor'kovskaia

Military carpenters built this very modest wooden cabin in three days in 1703. It was the first royal residence to be erected on the banks of the Neva in St. Petersburg, and one of the oldest structures in the city. Sitting on a bench outside, Peter watched his vision for this grand imperial city unfold. Early guides to St. Petersburg wrote pages questioning Peter's decision to build such a humble dwelling and went on to advise visitors to make this their first stop on their city tour, for "from this hut he, the Conqueror of Charles, forced arrogant Europe to respect him." It had exactly the effect Peter wished it to have, acquiring the status of a shrine where all could

*The dining room with a Russian-made oak table*

pay homage to the man. As such, it helped perpetuate the myth of unassuming modesty that Peter wished to promote.

Modeled on a traditional Russia *izba* (hut), it oddly combined features of a Dutch home with large and elaborate windows and a high roof covered with shingles. Originally the interior wooden walls were painted in red oil to imitate brick and thus they became known as the "red chambers." Keenly aware of the benefits of preserving things for posterity, Peter had a protective stone casing constructed around the cabin in 1723. Later Nikolai I, who considered Peter one of his heroes, funded a new brick outer casing, ventilation, and drainage channels. Placed under the protection of the Museums Authority in 1918, the cabin later became seen as an important architectural monument connected with the building of the city. When the Germans invaded the city and threatened to destroy it, the contents of the house were evacuated and the building was camouflaged to protect it from bombardment. Before heading to the front in 1944, soldiers took their oath here, swearing to fight for their country.

It was opened as a museum in 1930 and despite modifications and restoration over the years, it preserves the atmosphere it had from the years the tsar lived there between 1703 and 1708. Personal belongings, domestic items, and objects relating to the founding of the city and the construction and restoration of the house are divided among the study, dining room, and bedroom. Among these is a display describing the Russian naval victories against Sweden in the Northern War of 1700–21. Outside, mounted on a marble plinth is a bronze bust of Peter by the sculptor Parmen Zabello. Appropriately, it depicts him looking proudly out over the city.

*Bust of Peter the Great by Parmen Zabello*          **19**

# Museum of Toys
## Музей игрушки
## Muzei igrushki

6

**Address:** 32 Naberezhnaia reki Karpovki,
St. Petersburg 197022
**Tel:** 234-4312
**Open:** 11 A.M.–6 P.M., Tuesday to Sunday

**Metro:** Petrogradskaia
Please note that despite its address, the museum
is accessed via Ulitsa Vsevol'da Vishnevskogo,
opposite the Ioannovskii monastery

Russia is a country steeped in a rich array of folk art, from simple, functional objects produced by peasants and artisans for daily use in their homes, to highly carved and intricately painted articles, including dolls and other wooden or clay toys. Inspired by the continually changing environment that surrounds them, generations of folk artisans have been producing large numbers of ingenious toys, so it comes as a surprise that this is one of only two museums in Russia dedicated to preserving playthings. The other, much larger toy museum (over 30,000 objects) was first established in Moscow in 1918 and later moved to what is known as the "capital of the toy kingdom," Sergiev Posad, 45 miles (73 km) from the city. It was there that the first nesting dolls, known as Matrioshka dolls, were created in the 19th century. There too the craft of toymaking was established as a cottage industry, with thousands of artisans producing toys of all kinds.

The brainchild of Maria Marchenko, this museum was opened in 1997 as an independ-ently financed museum (i.e., not state-controlled). Since its inception Maria Marchenko has rapidly mustered a collection of over 3,000 items, primarily from Russia with a smattering of English and German-made items dating from 1860 through to the 1970s, including industrially manufactured toys. Most were purchased, but some been donated to the museum by local citizens. This museum not only prides itself on celebrating the cultural significance of Russian toys, but also acknowledges the special skills of the artisans and the aesthetics of their creations.

*A display of European dolls and toys*

*Selection of rocking horses*

They aim not only to collect, display, and study the collections not simply as unique historical items, but also as special forms of art in which ancient national traditions are intertwined with the most modern artistic trends. To achieve this the museum has become a "living museum," where master toymakers and other artists, including sculptors, designers, and painters, produce toys and objects associated with toys on the premises. Notable Russian contemporary artists who have worked here include the stone sculptor Lev Smorgon, who has also tried his hand at designing intricate toys, and the painter Victor Grigor'ev, who produced mechanical toys, among many others. A continually changing program of events for participants of all age groups has been built around these working artists.

The displays of toys are divided into three sections: folk, industrial, and *avtorskaia*, or those made by master artists. There is a large collection of theatrical wooden puppets, mostly dating from the 1930s–50s. Characters from popular fairy tales and works of literature hang alongside examples of the famed Petrushka, the minstrel clown whose story, set to music by Stravinsky, is among the best known in ballet. There are examples of the ubiquitous Matrioshka doll, one of the most popular gifts to bring back from Russia, as well as a good example of a 20th-century German dollhouse, one of the highlights of the collection. The unique display of over 300 dolls dressed in historic national costumes from different countries includes dolls from the regions of Russia. They date from various periods, and their clothing, made by master dollmakers from St. Petersburg, is based on historical documents. Recently, a fourth hall was opened for temporary exhibits, all related to toys and many originating from other museums. They have ranged from whimsical exhibits such as "Whistles" from the Bread Museum (see pp. 72–73), to "Serious Games" created by the Exhibition Center of the Union of St. Petersburg Artists.

*Matrioshka dolls and other traditional Russian toys*

**21**

# Academy of Arts Museum
Музей академии художеств
**Muzei akademii khudozhestv**

**7**

**Address:** 17 Universitetskaia Naberezhnaia,
St. Petersburg 199034
**Tel:** 213-3578
**Website:** www.museum.ru/M166

**Open:** 11 A.M.–6 P.M., Wednesday to Sunday
**Metro:** Vasileostrovskaia
**Further directions:** Bus 47 and tram 6 run from
the metro to the museum

Not far from the Naval Museum on the River Neva's Vassilievskii Island embankment stands the majestic Academy of Arts building, designed between 1764 and 1788 by the Russian architect Aleksandr Kokorinov and the Frenchman Jean-Baptiste Vallin de la Mothe. An imposing edifice, its façade is 459 feet (140 m) in length and is adorned with Doric columns on the lateral frontispieces and central portico. Pilasters run across the remainder of the façade. The building is 410 feet (125 m) deep, and four smaller rectangular courts at the corners form a round courtyard at its center. The Academy was originally meant to be built in Moscow as a place where Russian artists could be trained in the figurative arts. It was conceived by one of the figures of the Russian Enlightenment, Count I. I. Shuvalov, in 1757. However, it was not begun until Catherine II came to the throne and expressed a desire to show her commitment to the arts.

*The classically inspired main staircase*

The Academy's main purpose has always been to provide first-class training to gifted artists in painting, sculpture, architecture (it is the oldest architectural school in Russia), and engraving. To serve the students, a museum (as well as a scientific library) became part of the Academy. At first, items for the collection were mainly chosen for their educational value and for the purpose of copying, but later the museum became a repository for work of past masters across all disciplines, including those well known from Western schools, as well as for the work of both professors and students from the Academy. It now contains one of the best fine art collections in the country, with paintings dating from the mid-18th century to the present, plaster casts of classical and western European sculpture, an unsurpassed collection of architectural drawings (outstanding architects both studied and taught here), and wooden architectural models of some of the best buildings in the city including those by Carlo Rossi, the Smol'nii Convent built under the supervision of Bartolomeo Rastelli, and several by G. Quarenghi. A large selection of cork models of Roman monuments made by A. Chicchi in 1774 can also be seen.

Long hallways on the first floor link various galleries and spaces devoted to displays of sculpture and paintings. The roll call of painters includes the most famous graduates of the Academy such as the Russian realist painter Ilia Repin (after whom the Academy was renamed in 1944); the 18th-century court painter Dmitri Levitskii; the 18th-century portrait painter Orest Kiprenskii; and Karl Briullov, considered Russia's first master painter. They are matched by Russia's celebrated sculptors Mikhail Kozlovskii, a leading sculptor of Russian Classicism; Fiodor Shubin; and Stepan Pimenov. The second floor displays drawings and designs for buildings illustrating the progress of architectural art.

The Church of St. Catherine, built in the 1820s and named after the Academy's founder, has recently been restored. Opposite the Academy is a granite pier decorated with two Egyptian sphinxes that formerly graced the entrance to a temple built near Thebes. They were purchased and brought by ship to the city in the 1830s.

**23**

# Central Naval Museum
## Центральный военно-морской музей
### Tsentral'nii voenno-morskoi muzei

8

**Address:** 4 Birzhevaia Ploshchad,
  St. Petersburg 199034
**Tel:** 328-2502 / 328-2501
**Website:** www.museum.navy.ru
**Open:** 11 A.M.–6 P.M. Wednesday to Sunday;
  closed the last Thursday of every month
**Metro:** Sportivnaia, Vasileostrovskaia

**Further directions:** Bus 10 and trolleybus 7 run
  from Sportivnaia to the museum or take bus 47
  from Vasileostrovskaia to its final stop on
  Mendeleevskaia Linia, a few streets away from
  the museum
**Kiosk/shop, lecture/cinema hall, café/bar**

*The Stock Exchange Building housing the Naval Museum flanked by one of the Rostral Columns*

Peter the Great's compulsive, obsessive urge to do nothing by halves can hardly be seen better than here, at the Naval Museum founded in 1709 on his instructions. A larger-than-life character, his desire to gain access to the Baltic Sea and Baltic trade prompted him to establish the Russian Navy and along the way St. Petersburg, Russia's major seaport. And he did not stop there. In order to design his own vessels, he spent months working incognito in the shipyards of England and France learning shipbuilding trades. He also founded this collection, which today numbers 11,000 ship models and items of ship technology; 9,600 pieces of weaponry; more than 57,000 decorative works of art; and a startling 38,000 sailors' uniforms dating from the origins of the Russian fleet to the present day.

The collection started its life with ships' models from the Model Chamber of St. Petersburg Admiralty and the Admiralty Ship-Model

*Peter the Great's boat known as "Grandfather of the Russian Fleet"*

**25**

*Submarine by S. K Dzhevetskogo, 1880*

Chamber, where Peter deposited his models and working drawings of naval vessels. The collections expanded, necessitating a move in 1939 to what was once the original Stock Exchange building on Vasilevskii Island, designed by Thomas de Thomon between 1805 and 1816. Resembling a classical temple and appropriately decorated with stone sculptures of Neptune and Mercury, it is home to more than 600,000 items, a small fraction of which are displayed through 12 halls documenting the history of Russian seafaring. Two temporary halls extend the display space. For visitors short of time, it is advisable to take in only the main highlights.

Ship-model enthusiasts will be especially delighted by the most valuable models here, including the 100-cannon ship made in 1695 and donated to Peter by the English monarchs William III and his sister-in-law Anna Stuart; the Maltese galley from 1568, a French galley from the reign of Louis XIII; and the model frigate that Peter the Great crafted himself and called the "Grandfather of the Russian Navy."

Other significant collections include those of Russian, Soviet, and foreign orders and medals. In the archives one can find sketches of ships signed by Peter and other important figures of state and of the fleet. Also noteworthy are the thousands of banners, flags, war trophies, and personal effects of eminent commanders in the Russian Navy.

The museum also includes a whole arsenal of weapons and firearms dating from the Middle Ages, from swords and lances to pistols, blunderbusses, rifles, as well as machine guns, mines, and torpedos from the 20th century. The collection boasts personal weapons of famous admirals, such as the British Horatio Nelson; the Great Prince Konstantin Nikolaevich; and admirals of the Soviet fleet Kuznetsov and Gorshov. There are also the rare two-pound handgun, cast by Churkin in 1618, and the three-pound bronze cannon cast by Timofeevich in 1692.

The extensive library includes valuable editions from several centuries as well as literature about maritime themes from across the globe. It can be visited by appointment only.

Branches of the Central Naval Museum include: The Cruiser *Avrora*, the Submarine D-2 *Narodovolets*, Kronstadt Fortress, and "The Road of Life" on the banks of Lake Ladoga, whose exhibits tell the story of the Great Patriotic War and show conditions during the siege of Leningrad.

*The Russian fighter plane I-16 flown during the Second World War*

# D. I. Mendeleev Apartment-Museum & Archives

Музей-квартира и архивы Д.И. Менделеева

## Muzei-Kvartira i arkhivi D. I. Mendeleeva

**Address:** Gosudarstvennii Universitet Sankt Peterburga, 2 Mendeleevskaia Linia, St. Petersburg 199034

**Tel:** 328-9744 / 328-9737

**Website:** www.museum.ru/M124

**Open:** daily 11 A.M.–4 P.M. Monday to Friday; during the summer months visitors must book in advance

**Metro:** Vasileostrovskaia

**Further directions:** Bus 47 runs from the metro to its final stop on Mendeleevskaia Linia

*The study of D. I. Mendeleev at the University*

1874 he designed a more accurate balance for his research on gases and had it made in Paris. It is now displayed in the museum.

In 1866, following A. A. Voskresenskii, founder of the Russian Chemical Research School, Mendeleev moved into this apartment and lived and worked here until 1890. Four years after his death, the university and the Russian Chemical Society purchased these collections from his widow. They include his personal library and archives. Most of the apartment is not original, except for Mendeleev's study and the living room, where every week he entertained well-known painters, scientists, and poets.

As someone well versed in so many scientific disciplines, it's not surprising that Mendeleev's library consisted of about 20,000 titles in almost every branch of knowledge. Displayed here are Mendeleev's own works published during his lifetime, including his textbook *The Principles of Chemistry* and a special photocollage he made which he called *The Strengtheners of Periodic Law*. It consists of photos of the chemists credited with the discovery of the elements Mendeleev predicted.

This Russian genius of chemistry not only managed to set out the periodic table listing elements that had been discovered, but where gaps existed predicted the properties of missing elements and proudly lived to see three of them filled. It was in this apartment, designated for the professor of chemistry at the university, that Dmitri Mendeleev (1834–1907) produced some of his most important scientific writings and in 1869 discovered periodic law and constructed the periodic table, considered his greatest achievement. His research extended beyond this, however, he also did important work in the fields of meteorology, aerostatics, gases, and even economics, serving as a Russian government adviser in finance. In

Mendeleev worked standing at a bureau, on top of which now sit copies of his first sketches of the periodic table.

Albums arranged systematically by Mendeleev hold over 15,000 documents, manuscripts and drafts, letters, diaries, notebooks, and laboratory registers, among other items. In addition there is a collection of scientific instruments and other items belonging to his family.

**29**

# Peter the Great Museum of Anthropology and Ethnography (Kunstkammer)

Музей Антропологии и Этнографии им. Петра Великого (Кунсткамера)

**Muzei antropologii i etnografii im. Petra Velikogo (Kunstkamera)**

**10**

**Address:** 3 Universitetskaia Naberezhnaia,
St. Petersburg 199034
**Tel:** 328-1412
**Website:** www.kunstkamera.ru
**Open:** 11 A.M.–5:45 P.M.; closed Mondays
and the last Wednesday of every month.

**Metro:** Vasileostrovskaia, Sportivnaia
**Further directions:** Bus 10 and trolleybus 7 run
from Sportivnaia to the museum, or take bus 47
from Vasileostrovskaia to its final stop on
Mendeleevskaia Linia, a short way from
the museum

### *Including the* M. V. Lomonosov Museum
Музей М.В. Ломоносова  **Muzei M. V. Lomonosova**

*The Russian Academy of Sciences, library, and Kunstkammer*

Established by Peter the Great in 1714 as a vehicle to educate and transform the Russian people, the *Kunstkammer,* or "cabinet of wonders", is crammed full of natural and human oddities —from a baby with eyes under its nose and ears below its neck to other "monsters"—as well as artificial rarities, coins, minerals, and stuffed elephants and lizards. Also displayed are the tools Peter used to produce wooden and ivory objects, his surgical tools, and a collection of teeth he extracted himself from those whose teeth took his fancy. Peter's wish was to display these marvels so that the Russian people would look and learn in order to become "modern, civilized" people. And to assist him in building such a scientific collection that would rival those abroad, he demanded that everyone join in, with rewards based on a sliding scale for live or pickled specimens of birds, humans, or animals—the "very weird" commanding the largest payments. The fruits of all this madness are a collection that is truly encyclopedic in scope, reflecting the scientific and medical spirit of the 18th century. During this time of scientific revolution, learned Europeans were not only eager to share the wonders of their collections, but also saw them as a means of explaining the world around them to others and thus acknowledging the power of empirical discoveries. Today, these displays acquired by Peter continue to delight, inspire, and shock. No visitor to the city should miss this extraordinary museum, which says so much about Peter's world and the period of his reign.

Located on the banks of the River Neva in the center of the city, this first Russian museum of science was originally housed in the Summer Palace (Peter and Catherine's first proper residence in the city, begun in 1710). In 1726, a year after Peter's death, it was moved to a specially commissioned building on the spit of Vasilievskii Island. Here it held not only a library of rare volumes, but also the St. Petersburg Academy of Sciences, which later became known as the Russian Academy of Sciences. In its Anatomical Theater, like the one in Leiden and others elsewhere in Europe, the "new" science of anatomy, with its public dissections, astonished scientists of the day; the observatory and laboratories were packed with the first Russian scientists. Early in the 19th century the Academy established a

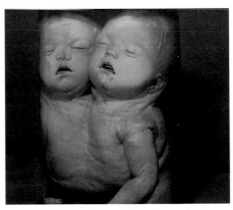

*Conjoined twins, 18th century, from the Ruysch collection*   **31**

*A 19th-century funeral headpiece worn by the Yaka people of the southwestern Congo, Africa*

number of additional museums (botanical, zoological, mineralogical, and ethnographical, among others) using the rich collections that had been gathered by scientists on their expeditions or accumulated from private individuals. Two of these museums, the Museum of Ethnography and the Museum of Anatomy, merged in 1878 to form the Museum of Anthropology and Ethnography. The new museum was named after its founder, Peter the Great, in 1903 and is known by that name today.

As the name suggests, the museum collections include assemblages of objects gathered from places far and wide. Peter sent expeditions not only to collect facts about the geology, botany, and geography of different places, but also to amass "priceless treasures" from Africa, China, North America, Southeast Asia, India, and elsewhere. Among the notable collections are those gathered by Gerhard Friedrich Müller, who spent ten years in Siberia; those of the herbalist Franz Luka Yelachich, who explored China; and the exceptional collection of Mongolian items, unparalleled in any other Russian museum. Sitting gracefully among these is the hall displaying what is left after the ravages of fire and ignorance of the scientific and historical value of Peter's rich stock, including prized items from a unique collection of several thousand specimens relating to human anatomy purchased from Frederik Ruysch, the celebrated Dutch anatomist. There are also zoological specimens from the German-born apothecary Albertus Seba, bought in Amsterdam in 1716; and shells, minerals, and stones from the cabinet of the physician Gottwald of Danzig. As Tolstoi said of Peter's

*The Hall of Australia and Oceania*

collection, it contains "the start of everything."

Occupying the tower and the circular hall on the upper floor of the museum is the **Lomonosov Museum**, established to commemorate the great Russian polymath Mikhail Lomonosov (1711–65). Educated in Germany, he returned to St. Petersburg and joined the Academy in 1741. He worked in this building cataloging and organizing the collections of the *Kunstkammer* and conducting research in a range of scientific fields. He contributed to geology, astronomy, metallurgy, and other disciplines, as well as to the arts, in particular poetry and the creation of mosaics. Hailed as Russia's first outstanding scholar and scientist, he went on to found Moscow University, which today bears his name.

At the center of the museum's main hall is a large round table, the one where the first Russian academicians gathered and held their meetings. Rooms off the hall display a selection of Lomonosov's personal possessions, manuscripts, and portraits of him. The museum's assets number some 3,785 items, including mosaics; over 300 exceptional Russian and foreign scientific instruments, and important decorative art objects, such as rare examples of Russia's first porcelain, developed by D. Vinogradov. The gem, however, is the Great Globe-Planetarium of Gottorp, created in 1654 in the Castle of Gottorp, the residence of the Duke of Holstein. No ordinary globe, it had a diameter of 10 feet (3.1 m), and 12 people could sit inside. Given as a gift to Peter I, it was installed in the *Kunstkammer* in 1726, only to be destroyed by fire in 1747. Recreated in 1748 with the surviving metal framing and door, it has a map of the night sky painted inside.

*Portrait of M. Lomonosov, Leontii Miropolskii, 1787*

*The Round Hall displaying the first items in Peter's Kunstkammer*

**33**

# Submarine D-2
## Д-2 Народоволец
## D-2 *Narodovolets*

**Address:** 10 Skiperskii Protok, St. Petersburg 199106
**Tel:** 356-5277
**Website:** www.museum.navy.ru
**Open:** 10 A.M.–6 P.M., Wednesday to Sunday;
  closed the last Thursday of every month

**Metro:** Primorskaia
**Further directions:** Buses 7 and 128 and trolleybus
  10 run from the metro to the intersection of
  Skiperskii Protok and Nalichnaia Ulitsa
**Kiosk/shop**

The gifted Russian engineer Boris M. Malinin, who proved his worth in constructing the BARS Type submarines in 1916–17, was also the principal designer of this diesel-electric submarine. It was one of six in a series that were named in memory of members of various revolutionary organizations. *Narodovolets* were members of the People's Will organization, a terrorist socialist group established in 1879. In 1933 this became one of the first submarines of the Soviet Northern Fleet, and a year later was renamed D-2 according to a new system of identification. The D-2 saw service during the Great Patriotic War under the command of Roman V. Lindenberg, and its success earned its crew a stream of medals and decorations for

heroism. It was later used for training missions until the 1980s, when the Soviet government decided to create a memorial to the history of submarine building and the Russian submarine fleet.

Displays of original armaments, communication equipment, and everyday objects are complemented by an exhibit focusing on the development of Soviet submarine technology, their engineers, and their successes in combat.

**34**

*Submarine D-2 in dry dock*

# Zoological Museum
## Зоологический музей
## Zoologicheskii muzei

**Address:** 1 Universitetskaia Naberezhnaia,
St. Petersburg 199034
**Tel:** 328-0112
**Website:** www.zin.ru
**Open:** 11 A.M.–6 P.M.; closed Fridays and
national holidays

**Metro:** Sportivnaia, Vasileostrovskaia
**Further directions:** Bus 10 and trolleybus 7 run
from Sportivnaia to the museum, or take bus 47
from Vasileostrovskaia to its final stop on
Mendeleevskaia Linia, a short walk from the museum
**Kiosk/shop**

Although the museum officially opened in 1832, its collections go back to Peter the Great, who bought zoological specimens from collectors in other countries for his *Kunstkammer,* or "cabinet of curiosities" (see pp. 30-33). His collection was part of his grand plan to educate the Russian people at a time when learned people created these "cabinets" as evidence of their inquiring minds and to help explain the mysteries of the natural world. Over the years specimens were continually added to Peter's core collection. When the museum's first inventory was prepared in 1742, it listed approximately 4,000 natural specimens. During the 18th century man's desire to learn more about the world meant scientific expeditions were sent out to collect not only information, but also zoological specimens. These were added to the museum until Peter's "room of wonder" was bursting at the seams. It was at this point that he wisely decided to establish specialized museums to contain all the precious specimens. The zoological museum was one of these.

*Arctic mammals*

**35**

*The baby mammoth, Dima*

the evolution of vertebrates and invertebrates, with special sections devoted to fishes, amphibians, reptiles, and birds. Among the collection of extinct animals there are the unique collections of Palearctic animals, including the Adams mammoth skeleton, which is one of the largest and most complete to be seen anywhere. This 44,000-year-old mammoth was discovered in the permafrost of Yakutia in 1903. Other finds include the most famous of all mammoths, the Berezovka mammoth, discovered in 1901 in Siberia, along with a baby mammoth (named Dima) found by miners encased in ice in 1977.

Today, it's run under the auspices of the Zoological Institute of the Russian Academy of Sciences and is located in converted warehouses on the spit of Vasilievskii Island, where it is housed along with the Zoological Institute. The collections have grown to comprise 40,000 animals and 15 million specimens. Even though the displays are densely packed (there are more than 30,000 exhibits) and captions are generally brief and mostly only in Russian, the exhibitions are well organized into two main sections. The first are the systematic displays of all the groups of the animal world. Upstairs, the visitor is confronted with the skeleton of a blue whale and models of polar bears and other Arctic life. The side hall traces

The second section consists of some outstanding dioramas showing groups of animals in their natural habitats, including Amur tigers and a nesting colony of emperor penguins. As the collections continue to grow through the work of scientists in the Institute, new exhibits are added to reflect their work. A new diorama entitled "Lions" has recently opened; "Giraffes in the Savannah" is due to follow soon.

The library of the Zoological Institute is also crammed with important volumes and engravings, from those formerly in the library of the museum's first director, Johann Friedrich Brandt, as well as those in the library of Peter the Great. Brandt began the tradition of passing their most valuable book collections to the library. The result is a growing collection of valuable sources that currently numbers over a half million items.

# History of Religion Museum
Музей истории религии
## Muzei istorii religii

**Address:** 14 Pochtamtskaia Ulitsa,
St. Petersburg 190000
**Tel:** 311-0495
**Website:** www.relig-museum.ru
**Open:** 11 A.M.–6 P.M.; closed Wednesdays

**Metro:** Nevskii Prospect
**Further directions:** Trolleybuses 5 and 22 run from the metro to the intersection of Pochtamtskaia Ulitsa and Voznesenskii Prospect.

*A ritual accessory used in shamanism*

Religious objects can be seen in museum collections throughout the world, but there are only a handful of museums devoted to the history of religion in its various guises. Since its establishment in 1932, the museum has amassed a collection that numbers more than 360,000 items, including paintings, books, sculptures, icons, and cult items relating to all sorts of different religions dating from ancient times up to the present day.

Since its inception, it has had a rather difficult time, sharing the fate of the country. Following a petition of the Presidium of the Academy of Sciences of the USSR the museum opened on November 15, 1932, in the Kazan Cathedral and was given its current name. This coincided with the announcement of Russia's first atheistic five-year plan. As religious persecution became more and more militant, the museum became a haven, particularly for the preservation of items belonging to cults that would otherwise have been destroyed. During the Second World War museum employees played a part in the safeguarding of the objects and its unique library. During this period the cathedral took on another role, serving as a hospital for the wounded and as a point of departure for soldiers who would swear their oath on the grave of the Russian military leader Prince M. Kutuzov, who was buried there in 1813. In 1954, the museum was renamed the Museum

**37**

*Displays tracing the history of the Russian Orthodox church*

of Religion and Atheism, aligning it with state policies that encouraged atheism among its citizens. While it continued to compile the collection and conduct scholarly research, its new role was as a propaganda machine. It was not until *perestroika* that the museum reverted to its original title. After an interval of over 60 years, on November 4, 1990, the cathedral held a service, and the following year, with the agreement of the museum's management, regular church services were resumed.

The museum opened in its present location in 2001 and has since then been on a program of refurbishment that includes the opening of new exhibition spaces and displays. The first year saw new halls dedicated to ancient beliefs and rites from shamanism to the religions of the ancient world (ancient Egypt, Greece, and Rome); Judaism; the birth of Christianity; and the history of Russian

Orthodoxy. The fascinating garments and artifacts of the Siberian shaman reflect their strong connection with nature and spirits. This archaic magical-religious practice uses a shaman and his magical powers to access higher realms and bring about a faith in universal unity through ecstatic experience. Shamanism, still practiced today in many religions throughout the world, has been practiced for millennia by the native peoples of Central Asia, Siberia, and the circumpolar region of the Northern Hemisphere. The hall dedicated to Russian Orthodoxy displays lavishly embroidered Russian Orthodox priests' garments and icons painted by the contemporary icon artist Vasnetsov executed in the style of older religious paintings.

To celebrate its 70th anniversary in November 2002, the museum opened a new section on Catholicism, which recounts the 2,000-year history of the western Christian church. Among the most interesting items displayed are the unique edition of *Malleus Maleficarum* first published in 1486 as a guidebook for Inquisitors during the Inquisition; the sculptures of *St. Louis—King of France, St. Florian*, and *Apostle Peter on the Papal Throne*; and the collection of papal medals, cult cups, and other items.

In the near future halls will be opened dedicated to the history of Protestantism, so that visitors to the museum will be presented with the whole spectrum of the history of Christianity. There are also plans to reintroduce the exhibits dedicated to the Western Middle Ages, a large part of which concerns the Inquisition, which has been absent from display for 20 years. Rooms on Buddhism and Islam are also planned.

# Museum of Russian Vodka
## Музей русской водки
### Muzei russkoi vodki

**Address:** 5 Konnogvardeiskii Bul'var,
  St. Petersburg 190068
**Tel:** 312-9178
**Website:** www.vodkamuseum.ru/museum
**Open:** 11 A.M.–10 P.M. daily

**Metro:** Nevskii Prospect, Gostinii Dvor
**Further directions:** Buses 3, 22, and 27 and
  trolleybuses 5 and 22 run from the metro to
  the museum
**Restaurant, souvenir shop**

Quintessentially Russian, this distilled alcohol diluted with water was most likely inspired by the strong drink called *aqua vitae* first brought to Russia by Genoese merchants in the 14th century. This fermented grape juice was largely ignored until the next century, when it was again brought to Russia for medicinal purposes. It was then that the Russian monk Zosima got the idea of distilling a version from grain. The rest is history.

By the beginning of the 16th century Russia was exporting its famous product, but at home Ivan the Terrible enforced a state monopoly over the drink. By setting up *kabaks*, or taverns, he controlled the sale of the drink to ordinary Russians. These inns became crowd-pullers where people drank themselves sick, played dice, fought, and plotted against the state. History reveals variations not only in the production of the drink, but also in how it was sold. Catherine II allowed the nobility the privilege of producing vodka, and also abolished any related taxes. However, the start of the Patriotic War of 1812 plunged the government into debt, and a state monopoly on its production was enforced yet again.

*A selection of vodka labels*

**39**

Tracking the long history of this country's most famous product reveals a great deal about Russia's social and economic history, not to mention its language and folklore. Vodka became a necessary combat ration for soldiers, who were allocated two shots daily. The legendary drinking feats at feasts and banquets are awe-inspiring. Recorded deaths from drinking vodka in the mid-19th century rose to 1,000 a year and became a threat to national life. The prohibition introduced in 1914 made the problem even worse, with Russians drinking paraffin and other dangerous, illegal concoctions; the loss of tax revenues is believed to have contributed to the government's downfall in 1917.

Despite its sometimes-negative image, vodka is an essential part of Russian life. This museum—the only one in Russia dedicated to the drink—tells the story of vodka's role in Russian history from the early centuries right up to the present day. It accomplishes this brilliantly through its collection of vodka bottles dating back to the 1860s, shot glasses, labels, posters, and relating memorabilia. Some of the more unusual phenomena connected with the drink are explained through illustrative material, including the rule, dating back to Peter the Great's time, saying that anyone who was late arriving at a feast had to drink a bowl full of vodka or face a fine. A very special item in the museum is one of the original bottles for the famous "Moscow Special" vodka, which became the official Russian national drink when it was patented in 1894. Its invention was the work of

*Cases with items tracing the history of vodka*

the chemist D. I. Mendeleev, who discovered the ideal volume-to-weight ratio of water to alcohol, thus establishing the national standard. The collection also houses some of the very first distillation devices, explains the uses of various-sized bottles and the fact that before 1885 vodka was sold only in 13-quart (12.3 l) buckets, and devotes a portion of its displays to the Great Patriotic War and the introduction of the daily ration of vodka for front-line soldiers, known as the "Commissar's 100 Grams." Labels from many of the more famous brands, such as *Russkii Standart* ("Russian Standard") and *Stolichnaia* ("Capital") are also displayed.

The restaurant offers an assortment of the best vodkas along with Russian snacks, including caviar, salmon, pickled and marinated cucumbers, and mushrooms.

# V. V. Nabokov Museum
## Музей В.В. Набокова
## Muzei V. V. Nabokova

**Address:** 47 Ulitsa Bolshaia Morskaia,
  St. Petersburg 190000
**Tel:** 311-4502
**Website:** www.nabokov101.ru
**Open:** 11 A.M.–6 P.M. daily, except Fridays
  10 A.M.–5 P.M.; closed Mondays

**Metro:** Nevskii Prospect, Gostinii Dvor
**Further directions:** Trolleybuses 5 and 22 run
  from the metro to their final stop at Ploshchad'
  Truda, a short walk from the museum
**Lecture/cinema hall, public library**

This splendid three-story Art Nouveau build-ing was once the townhouse of the Nabokov family. It was here that Vladimir Nabokov (1899–1977), the famous writer, chess player, and butterfly collector, was born and lived for the first 18 years of his life, before the Bolsheviks forced the family into exile. This home, along with the family estate near Vira, outside St. Petersburg, was the setting for many of Nabokov's novels and for his autobiography, *Speak, Memory*, in which he describes his happy childhood lovingly and with obvious nostalgia. Though the house was taken over by the Red Guard after the Revolution it was never turned into communal apartments and parts of the original layout and designs can still be seen.

Opened in 1998, the museum occupies the first floor of the house and is run as a non-profit organization. This floor, originally was known as the "family floor," held a dining room, living room, a room for political meet-ings run by his father (V. D. Nabokov, a

*Nabokov collecting butterflies in Switzerland*

**41**

well-known liberal lawyer), a library, and a kitchen. Little memorabilia from Nabokov's time here remains, but some of the original room details, such as the well-preserved library (which once housed 10,000 volumes), with its carved oak ceiling and door, can be admired. The heart of the house, the library was also a gathering place for writers, politicians, musicians, and other celebrities. Since the museum opened, donations of books, printed material, photographs, and documents illustrating Nabokov's childhood and youth, his life and art, the history of the family and their many homes have poured in from those eager to preserve his memory.

Also on display are several original pieces of furniture, books from the family library, and paintings, as well as some of Nabokov's personal belongings, such as his pince-nez, pencils, and index cards, and even a small section of his extensive butterfly collection presented to the museum by Harvard University.

Tours of the Nabokov family estates near St. Petersburg and in the city itself are available for those who want to learn more about the author and his life. Contact the museum for details, or visit their website.

*Exterior of the Art Nouveau town house, now the V.V. Nabokov Museum*

# A. S. Pushkin Apartment-Museum
Музей-квартира А.С. Пушкина
**Muzei-kvartira A. S. Pushkina**

**16**

**Address:** 12 Naberezhnaia Moiki,
  St. Petersburg 191186
**Tel:** 314-0007
**Website:** www.museumpushkin.ru
**Open:** 10:30 A.M.–5.00 P.M.; closed Tuesdays
  and the last Friday of every month

**Metro:** Nevskii Prospect
**Further directions:** Buses 3, 7, 22, and 27 and
  trolleybuses 1, 5, 7, 10, and 22 run from the metro
  to the bridge on Nevskii Prospect over the Moika.
**Kiosk/shop, lecture/cinema hall, public library**

This is the most visited literary museum in St. Petersburg, containing the largest repository (numbering around 10,000 items) of relics, books, and works of art connected with the life of Russia's greatest poet. The former Volkonskii House (having belonged to the family of Prince Volkonskii from 1806) was Aleksandr Pushkin's last residence before he was killed in a duel in 1837 at Chornaia Rechka. Built in the 1720s, the house has been restored to look as it did when Pushkin lived and worked here, editing his journal *The Contemporary* and finishing *The Captain's Daughter*.

The museum on the ground floor is centered on Pushkin's memorial apartment where he lived in 1836–37 with his wife, four children, his wife's two sisters, and some 15 staff members. One can visit the poet's study, where a number of his possessions are on display, including such personal items as a decanter and wine glass, walking sticks, scissors, a pipe, and an inkwell. There is a fine collection of works of art, including a number of portraits of Pushkin. In addition, there are hundreds of portraits of the poet's contemporaries done by the great masters of the period, pictures depicting events in Pushkin's life, illustrations for his works, and items of decorative art. New displays feature the dress shoes of Pushkin's wife, Natalia, which she supposedly wore on their wedding day; there is also a showroom with two exhibitions dedicated to the history of the house at Moika. The museum's archives consist of thousands of rare publications, many of which bear the autographs of Pushkin's contemporaries.

Pushkin is the national poet of Russia, and this museum is a veritable shrine to his work and life. People from all strata of society lined the streets and packed the church to attend his funeral. Such was the prestige of Pushkin—the author of such works as *Ruslan and Liudmila* (1820), *Boris Godunov* (1826), and *Eugene Onegin* (1831)—that even the tsar wrote to him before

**43**

*Pushkin's study in his house on the Moika River*

he died. Following this wave of nationwide grief, appropriate emphasis is placed on his death too. The clock in his study, where he spent his last hours before the duel, shows the exact time of his death. Visitors can also see the waistcoat he wore as he lay bleeding in the snow, complete with bullet hole. Another display case holds a candle from the funeral and a glove worn by his friend Viazemskii; the matching glove was placed in the poet's coffin.

On the second and third floors of this same building is the exhibit "Aleksandr Pushkin, Life and Work." Although the exhibit was created in 1938, it was only moved to this address in 1999. It covers events in his personal and professional life and includes his birth certificate, short pieces of his work, engravings and lithographs, and rare editions of his books. Many pieces of furniture in the exhibit are originals which were used by the poet himself. The armchair was brought to this museum from his family estate in Mikhailovskoe, and the writing desk brought from his country estate in Boldino. The collection contains possessions of friends and contemporaries of the poet, including the writing desk of the author Nikolai Karamzin (1766–1826), at which he sat to write his book *The History of the Russian State.*

The All-Russian Pushkin Museum is an umbrella for five branches (see separate entries).

# Central Museum of Railway Transport

Центральный музей железнодорожного транспорта

**Tsentral'nii muzei zheleznodorozhnogo transporta**

**17**

**Address:** 50 Sadovaia Ulitsa,
St. Petersburg 190068
**Tel:** 315-1476 / 168-8005
**Website:** www.museum.ru/M171
**Open:** 11 A.M.–5.30 P.M., Sunday to Thursday;
closed the last Thursday of every month

**Metro:** Sadovaia, Sennaia Ploshchad'
**Two branches: The Museum of National Bridge Construction** (Mostotrud 19 building, Prospect Lenina 77, Krasnoe Selo, St. Petersburg) and **Open yard at Lebazie Station**, which can be viewed by appointment only

This museum is for model railway enthusiasts. Among the oldest technical museums in the world, its core collection originates from the St. Petersburg Institute of Engineers' Communication Networks, formed in 1813, which amassed and housed models and documents about the most remarkable engineering structures in Russia. The institute's students used these as study aids, and the engineers who worked on their construction are responsible for many of them. The models of railways, railroad structures, and bridges built before the Revolution are particularly beautiful, intricately constructed in brass, wood, and other fine materials; they are exceptional works of art made by masters of carpentry and metalwork. The collection was used solely for research purposes until 1862, when it was opened to the public. The collection grew as models continued to be added, and in 1902 a specially built museum by P. Kupinskii was commissioned. This is where the collection is housed today.

Visitors have over 11 large halls to explore, with displays showing a small proportion of the collection, which numbers well over 55,000 items. The exhibits are arranged thematically, starting with the building of the first railroads; the history of bridge-building for the railways; the development of rolling stock (locomotives, diesel locomotives, electric locomotives, wagons); track and rail maintenance; and the implementation of signaling and links on railroads. Most fascinating are displays linked with the development of railroads—from wooden and cast iron factory railroads to railroads for general use. There is a 1:2 scale model of the first Russian steam engine, built by the Cherepanovs (father and son mechanics) in 1834, and a model of the English steam engine *Provornii* ("Quick" or "Swift") built by students of the Technological Institute in 1839. This steam engine was sent for in 1838 to run on the first Russian railroad for general use between St. Petersburg and the imperial palaces Tsarskoe

*Model of the first St. Petersburg to Moscow railway*

Selo and Pavlovsk, south of the city.

The exhibit dedicated to the **Institute of Engineers' Communication Networks**—the first higher education institute of transportation in Russia, founded in 1809—displays early models built by this institute. The models of bridges showing the development of bridge-building in Russia should not be missed. On display is an impressive wooden model of the bridge over the Yenisei River in Siberia, designed by I. P. Proskouriakov, and the cast iron one by K. P. Berd at Salnii Bouian in St. Petersburg. The archives hold one of the most interesting models of a chain bridge over the River Dnieper in Kiev, built in 1853 and presented to Tsar Nikolai I by the London master, Vinol.

A separate exhibit tells of the building of the longest main line—the Great Siberian Route (1891–1901). Items relating to this were shown in the Universal Exhibition in Paris in 1900 and are now kept mostly in the museum storeroom.

In the hall on the development of the Russian steam locomotive and their coaches, there is a model of the train that traveled between St. Petersburg and Moscow, showing how the first steam engines and their passenger and freight cars looked in the middle of the 19th century. The first passenger cars in first and second class had soft, cushioned seats, and movable back-rests that allowed passengers to sit either face to face or in the direction in which the train was traveling. The model of the Trans-Siberian Express that went from Moscow to Irkutsk in 1900 holds particular interest. This train had very comfortable first- and second-class carriages, a saloon car, and a special car with extra seating for the long journey to eastern Siberia.

The museum's archives hold unique albums with photographs, drawings, and related items, such as medals and coins, connected with the construction of the railroads.

There are two other branches. The first is the **Museum of National Bridge Construction** (Mostotrud building 19, 77 Prospect Lenina, Krasnoe Selo, St. Petersburg), which is unique in Russia and tells of the development of bridge-building in St. Petersburg and of railroad bridges across the country. Besides displaying models of bridges, the walls are hung with portraits of the engineers and scientists who were the founders of Russian bridge construction. The second branch is the **open in a yard on Lebazie Station**, where there is a collection of over 50 working locomotives from the 19th and the beginning of the 20th century. Call for opening times.

# History of Printing Museum
## Музей истории печати Muzei istorii pechati
## A branch of The State Museum of The History of St. Petersburg

**Address:** 32/2 Naberezhnaia reki Moiki,
 St. Petersburg 191186
**Tel:** 238-4658 / 311-0270 / 312-0977
**Open:** 11 A.M.–6 P.M. daily, except Tuesdays
 11 A.M.–4 P.M., and Fridays 11 A.M.–5 P.M.;

closed Wednesdays
**Nearest metro:** Nevskii Prospect
**Further directions:** Buses 3 and 7 and trolleybuses
 1, 5, 7, and 10 run from the metro to the Moika
Bridge on Nevskii Prospect.

Prior to the printing of the first newspaper *Novosti* ("The News") in Russia by the Moscow Printing House in 1702, publications were mainly limited to those produced by the church or, on rare occasions for the government. Less than a decade later, St. Petersburg set up presses to produce their first newspaper, *Russkaia Gazeta* ("The Russian Gazette") This museum, housed in an old printing house built in 1905, is devoted not only to this early period of printing, but also to the history of printing in St. Petersburg at the beginning of the 20th century, prior to the Revolution. This was a time when great political turmoil thundered through Russia and publications played an important role as "the voice of the people."

This apartment, located on the second floor, originally housed the editorial office and printing presses for the publishers of the government paper *Selskii Vestnik* ("Rural Bulletin"). Later, in 1917, the Bolshevik newspaper *Pravda* ("Truth," first published in April 1912) resumed publication here in March for five

months before its demise in July that same year, churning out 99 editions. During this period it was under the editorship of Lenin, who had returned from exile in Poland. The museum was founded in 1984 and until 1991 was called "Lenin and the Paper *Pravda*."

*Lenin's office where he worked as editor on* Pravda

**47**

The museum is split into two parts, separated by a hallway. The first section consists of four rooms, which include the editorial offices of the newspaper. Here, the original atmosphere is recreated using photographs taken at the time; the rooms are bathed in dim light and the tables covered with old newspapers, editorial paraphernalia, and typographic equipment. Next door is the editor's office, where, Lenin wrote approximately 160 articles for the paper as well as speeches. The other two rooms house exhibits—one on the history of the paper, from 1912–17, and another on pre-Revolutionary activities.

The second half of the museum has two rooms. One is dedicated to printing techniques from the end of the 17th century to the 19th century. The alteration of the Cyrillic alphabet during the time of Peter the Great is explained here. Before Peter, Church Slavonic (with 36 letters) was the official language of Russia. Peter, however, modified the language, altering it to a version with 32 letters to make it more accessible to the populace as a whole. The room is divided to show the main differences between the two alphabets. Next to it is a room with large windows housing the printing presses used to print *Pravda*. (By prior arrangement, these can be used to demonstrate printing techniques.)

The museum is difficult to find. It is housed on the second floor of an apartment building on the banks of the Moika River. If no one answers the door, ask at apartment 1 in the building to gain access.

*Historic printing presses used to print* Pravda

# Museum of Circus Art
## Музей циркового искусства
### Muzei tsirkovogo iskusstva

**Address:** 3 Naberezhnaia reki Fontanki,
  St. Petersburg 191011
**Tel:** 313-4413
**Website:** www.museum.ru/M186
**Open:** 11 A.M.–6 P.M. Monday to Friday

**Metro:** Gostinii Dvor, Nevskii prospect
**Further directions:** Buses 3, 7, 22, and 27 and
  trolleybuses 1, 5, 7, 10, and 22 run from the
  metro to the bridge on Nevskii Prospect over
  the Fontanka

It's hard to miss this elegant, brightly colored building that sits on the Fontanka, surrounded by somewhat more conventional structures. Built in 1877 by the architect Vassilii Kenel, it was the first Russian stone building expressly designed for circus performances. The brainchild of the Italian circus performer, rider, and trainer Gaetano Chinizelli, head of a large circus family who first arrived in St. Petersburg in 1847, its impressive structure with statues of the muses in the arched open windows was considered one of the finest circus buildings in Europe. The interior was equally stunning, decorated with gilt, crimson velvet, and painted murals of circus acts. It once also had stables for the horses used in the popular riding acts and accommodation for the Chinizelli family, all of whom performed.

Chinizelli's Circus, as it was called before the Revolution, played an important role in the development of Russia's revered circus traditions.

*Watercolor of Chinizelli's circus building, 1877*

Many of the world's best performed here, including famous clowns, air gymnasts, and riders, and it was attended by everyone, including the aristocracy, who considered it fashionable. After the

*Poster celebrating the anniversary of the director of the Leningrad Circus, W. Truzzi*

Revolution the circus was transferred to the state, and the name was changed to the Leningrad Circus. The Soviet circus flourished during the 1920s and 1930s under the new director, W. Truzzi, who encouraged the creation of large-scale pantomimes using horses, fireworks, and waterfalls. Such creative vision was rewarded with the Order of the Red Banner of Labor, a vision that continued into the postwar period with the artistic achievements of an endless list of talented circus performers, including Valentin Filatov, who introduced "The Bear Circus," which continues to be one of the main attractions. Today the circus continues to entertain thousands of visitors a year.

Located inside this building is the museum's collection, an enormous cache of memorabilia recounting the famous Russian circus artists and the history of other domestic and foreign circuses. It opened in 1928 due to the foresight of P. Y Andreev, a fencing teacher in the Leningrad Theatrical Institute who was so passionate about the theatrical arts that he amassed everything related to it, and of the circus historian E. M. Kuznetsov. The collection suffered during the war, but was helped by the determined director, A. Z. Levin, who restored the building and expanded the collections. Over the years the collection grew with donations from leading Russian circus performers, such as Yurii Nikulin and Oleg Popov. Today it contains over 80,000 items. There's a vast collection of books, posters (including the one celebrating the former director, W. Truzzi), programs, commemorative medals, circus costumes and badges, as well as souvenir clown dolls and statuettes. The outstanding library contains more than 5,000 volumes, including many rare volumes on the circus from the end of the 18th century, and research documents undertaken by circus historians.

# Museum of Theatrical and Musical Arts
Музей театрального и музыкального искусства
## Muzei teatral' nogo i muzikal' nogo iskusstva

**20**

**Address:** 6 Ploshchad' Ostrovskogo,
  St. Petersburg 191011
**Tel:** 311-2195 / 310-1939
**Website:** www.museum.ru/M148

**Open:** 11 A.M.–6 P.M. daily, except: Wednesdays
  1 P.M.–7 P.M.; closed Tuesdays
**Metro:** Gostinii Dvor
**Lecture/cinema hall**

## State Museum of Theater and Music; Library
Государственный музей театрального и музыкального
### Gosudarstvennii muzei teatral' nogo i muzikal' nogo iskusstva Biblioteka

**Address:** 6 Ploshchad' Ostrovskogo,
  St. Petersburg 191011
**Tel:** 315-5243

The library is on the ground floor of the museum. It can be reached by using the main entrance of the museum. Please apply for special permission to access the archives and stacks.

Housed in one of the city's architectural masterpieces, begun in 1828 by Carlo Rossi, this museum was founded in 1918. Its collection numbers some 450,000 items and reflects the history of the performing arts in Russia from the 18th century through to the present day. Opened in 1922, it is housed on the third floor in the former Imperial Theater's administration building. The building forms part of the glorious Ostrovskii Square, which is dominated by the Alexandrinskii Theater, also built by Rossi and one of the largest theaters in the city. To fully experience Rossi's arrangement of the buildings laid out around the hexagonal-shaped square, approach the theater from the embankment of the Fontanka rather than from Nevskii Prospect. Before you will be one of the most stunning architectural views in the city.

Theater enthusiasts and those interested in the artistic heritage of Russia should make this museum one of their first stops. Although the displays are extensive, they are well laid out over three rooms (with an additional hall for performances and video viewings) arranged chronologically from tsarist times through to the pre- and post-Revolutionary periods, right up to the present day. The extensive holdings of theatrical costumes rank the collection among the largest in the world. These are complemented by numerous sculptures, models of

**51**

*Model of a post-Revolutionary avant-garde stage designed for Vsevolod Meierkhol'd*

stage sets, photographs, and personal belongings of such famous performers as the dancers Anna Pavlova (1881–1931) and A. Vaganova (1879–1951); the choreographer Mikhail Fokine (1880–1942); and the opera singer N. Figner (1887–1907), among others.

Upon entering the visitor is presented with two bejeweled costumes. Displayed within a darkened recess framed by stage curtains and a highly decorated backdrop, they featured in a performance of Tolstoi's *The Death of Ivan the Terrible*. They establish the grand tone of the museum's first room, with its high ceilings and chandeliers playing host to a fantastic array of theatrical memorabilia, reflecting a sense of theater-loving high society in the early days of Russian theater. Highlights include the vintage theatrical costumes and stage sets designed by many well-known artists, including Aleksandr Benois (1870–1960), who loved ballet, and his friend Leon Bakst (1866–1924). Both were members of the World of Art circle, a movement founded by artists in St. Petersburg to educate the public in the arts.

*Costumes designed for Tolstoi's*
The Death of Ivan the Terrible

In contrast to all this is the final room, though the room itself is by no means any less impressive. Its centerpiece is a smaller-scale model of a post-Revolutionary avant-garde stage designed by the Constructivist artist Liubov Popova for the theater director Vsevolod Meierkhol'd (1874–1940) in his 1922 production of the *Magnanimous Cuckold.* During this period the theater was designed as a living entity—an interactive part of the staging as a whole—and as such, stages were built as highly complex structures comprising numerous layers with stairways and ramps connecting them. Around this stage, the walls are hung with Soviet propaganda posters, reflecting the voice of Soviet ideology of the period, just as plays of that time reflected the strength of the Soviet machine and of the united proletariat. Another aspect of Soviet theater is reflected in the model of the street theater: theatrical spectacles took place outside and were performed by huge crowds of people, thus evoking a sense of the unified mass as opposed to the heroic individual of former times.

Complementing the displays are the museum's archives held in the **Theatrical Library**. Its core includes the directors' archives of the imperial theaters, and material from the personal archives of the choreographer Marius Petipa (1818–1910); the great baritone, Fedor Shaliapin (who rose to fame in Savva Mamontov's Private Opera, established in 1855, several years after the tsar lifted the private monopoly of the Imperial Theater), the letters of the composer Piotr Chaikovskii (1840–93); and the musical manuscripts of N. I. Rimskii-Korsakov (1844–1908). Sketches of costumes and decorations from various periods include those from artists of the 18th century up to the Constructivists, such as Vladimir Tatlin of the Soviet period, and beyond to modern times. An abundant collection of photographs and portraits includes famous figures of the Russian theatrical world, such as the writers Denis Fonvizin (1745–92; he wrote *The Brigadier,* among other comedies); Maxim Gorkii (1868–1936); Anton Chekhov (1860–1904); and the actor Konstantin Stanislavskii (1863–1938).

**53**

# National Library Museum
## (The National Library of Russia)
Музей Национальной Библиотеки
(Российская Национальная Библиотека)

### Muzei Natsional'noi Biblioteki (Rossiiskaia Natsional'naia Biblioteka)

**Address:** 18 Sadovaia Ulitsa,
  St. Petersburg 191069
**Tel:** 310-2856
**Website:** www.nlr.ru
**Open:** 9 A.M.–9 P.M. daily
**Metro:** Nevskii Prospect, Gostinii Dvor

**Metro:** Nevskii Prospect, Gostinii Dvor
Access to the library is by reader's ticket only.
However, tours of the library and its exhibits can
be arranged through the Public Relations Service
(OMR). Contact: 310-6875 or excibition@nlr.ru.
There is also a series of lectures and events.
Details of these can also be provided by the
Public Relations Service.

*A facsimile edition of the 15th century
Prayer Book of Louis d'Orléans*

Along the right-hand side of Ostrovskii Square is the Ionic-columned façade of the National Library of Russia, crowned with a figure of Minerva, goddess of wisdom, and decorated with statues of philosophers. This Carlo Rossi-built extension of St. Petersburg's first public library (first opened in 1814) now holds combined stocks of more than 32 million items, almost one-sixth of which are in foreign languages. Its rich collection of rare books includes Voltaire's library, which was purchased by Catherine the Great. It also boasts a postage-stamp-sized edition of Krilov's *Fables*, which is so clearly printed that it can be read with the naked eye. A plaque on the Nevskii side of the library attests that Lenin was a regular visitor here between 1893 and 1895.

The library is over 300 years old and is one of the largest book repositories in the world. It was founded by Catherine the Great as both a collection of Russian books and also as a library for public usage. Various statesmen and scholars have in the past frequented the museum, and for many, the library came to be known as a "second university." The "Depot of Manuscripts," established in 1805 after the Count Aleksandr Stroganov (one of the

*One of the rooms of the Manuscript Department*

library's former directors) obtained an outstanding manuscript collection, houses the oldest of Russian manuscript books, the *Ostromir Gospel* (1056–57) and the *Lavrentievskaia Chronicle* (1377), which contains the beginnings of Russian historiography. No less significant are the massive collections of Greek manuscripts, among which there are documents written on papyrus from the 2nd to 4th centuries. These are not to be outdone by the manuscripts from the East, or those from western Europe, including some 6,000 codices of the 15th–20th centuries. The valuable collection of 15th-century incunabulae is

beautifully arranged on ornate wooden shelves in the "Cabinet of Faust," designed to resemble a Gothic monastic library.

The library also owns a huge quantity of archive material, with more than 10,000 early Russian documents from 1269 to 1700, and deeds, memoirs, diaries, travel notes, and personal archives of notable cultural figures starting from the 18th century. There is a newspaper and periodical stock including thousands of titles from the Russian Empire and the Soviet Union. And their specialist stock contains the whole gamut of printed materials such as maps, atlases, photographs, posters, and engravings.

**55**

# Russian Ethnographic Museum
Российский Этнографический музей
## Rossiiskii Etnograficheskii muzei

**22**

**Address:** 4/1 Ulitsa Inzhenernaia,
  St. Petersburg 191011
**Tel:** 313-4421
**Website:** www.ethnomuseum.ru

**Open:** 10 A.M.–6 P.M.; closed Mondays and
  the last Friday of every month
**Metro:** Nevskii Prospect, Gostinii Dvor
**Kiosk/shop, lecture/cinema hall, café/bar**

The museum is housed in the east wing of the Mikhailovskii Palace, originally built by Carlo Rossi in 1819 for the Grand Duke Michael Pavlovich. When Nicholas II decided to establish the Russian Museum as a memorial to his father, Alexander III, and as a center of culture about and for the Russians, the architect Vassilii Svin'in got to work remodeling the palace. A brilliant draftsman and an artist with flair for proportions and materials, he built the expansive Marble Hall in the Greco-Roman architectural tradition. Twenty-eight rose-colored marble columns line the hall, and a glass ceiling sheds light onto the delicate bronze

*Marble Hall embellished with marble columns and Socialist Realist frieze*

*Interior of a yurt with models of Kazakhs,
late 19th–early 20th century*

openwork above the columns. Sculpted at the base is the high-relief Socialist Realist frieze of peasants and workers from every nationality of the former USSR by M. Kharlamov. The hall was originally built to house a bronze statue of Aleksandr III, but military and political events in the wake of the October Revolution hampered this plan. Today it grandly displays many treasures from the museum's vast collection. Additionally, Svin'in added the east wing to perpetuate the memory of Aleksandr III by "collecting everything relating to his personality and the history of his reign." The result is a remarkable collection numbering close to half a million objects, with displays of folk art, costumes, tools, reconstructed house interiors,

and photographs representing dozens of regional groups and nationalities. It offers a fascinating insight into the variety of people and cultures that once inhabited the Soviet Empire and beyond, including western and southern Slavs, the Finns, the Swedes, the Norwegians, the Chinese, the Persians, the Mongols, and others. Its collection of folk costumes is considered to be the most preeminent to be found anywhere, due to the Soviets' desire to collect costumes as proletarian artwork. Uniform in quality, the hall dedicated to the ethnic Russian peasant dress is outstanding.

The exhibits trace the peasant life of the Russian people, which was the norm for 90 percent of the population until the early 20th century. The visitor is shown numerous ethnic groups from the North Caucasus, such as the Chechens and Ingush, their Iranian neighbors, the Ossetians and Georgians. In an adjoining room are the numerous ethnic groups who live in the Volga basin and the Ural Mountains: the largest of these is Tartars (their robes with highly ornate embroidery are especially impressive), followed by the Bashkirs and Chuvash, the latter one of the few non-Muslim Turkic people. The Mordvinians, Udmurty, Mari, and Komi are also present here, representing the Finno-Ugric group. Furthermore, there are the few remaining nomadic Siberian Lapps, such as the Evenki and Nanaytsy, who still follow the movements of the reindeer. The more numerous Buriat people remained

*Female festive costume worn by the Setu Estonians*

nomads until after the Revolution, and traditionally practiced shamanism, but have since settled more or less permanently around Lake Baikal. The other main group represented here is the Iakuts, herders whose language and culture continue to thrive. Finally, there are, of course, also the more familiar western Slav people, beginning with the two largest groups, the Ukrainians and the White Russians or Belorussians, followed by the Estonians, Latvians, and Lithuanians. Additionally, the collection holds outstanding embroidered items of clothes and everyday life. The well-documented Central Asian carpet collections, built up systematically by leading Russian ethnographers of carpets and flatweaves, include flatwoven horse covers collected in 1902 by the Russian traveler and photographer S. Dudin. The unique treasury of jewelery (numbering 12,000 items) contains examples from the seven cultural-historical regions of jewelery production dating from the 17th to the 20th century. Full sets of jewelery worn with festive costumes are included. Massive silver clasps worn by the Baltic peoples and delicate gold filigree adornments of the Kazan Tartars vie for space with engraved ornamental jewelery from Turkmenistan and coral pendants that adorn the costumes of Buryat women.

The archives hold invaluable drawings, watercolors, and paintings depicting domestic dwellings, forms of transportation, tools, clothing, ornaments, and so on. One of the highlights are the drawings by I. G. Georgi depicting peoples of the Russian state in their native costumes printed in 1776–77.

Thousands of photographs taken from 1867 to 1999 document both the past and present Russian Empire, capturing a range of traditional activities and holidays. Manuscripts hold accounts of expeditions and unpublished research by museum workers, along with material in the "Ethnographical Bureau" established in 1895 to gather information about the culture of Russian peasants. There is also a library containing almost all publications about Russian ethnography and other people published in Russian during the 19th and 20th centuries.

# Zoshchenko Museum
## Музей М.М. Зощенко
### Muzei M.M. Zoshchenko

**23**

**Address:** Apartment 119, 4/2 Ulitsa Malaia
 Konniushennaia, St. Petersburg 191186
**Tel:** 311-7819
**Website:** www.museum.ru/M135

**Open:** The museum was under repair when this
 book went to print; please call to find out
 opening times.
**Metro:** Nevskii Prospect

Hugely popular with the people of Russia in the 1920s and 1930s, Zoshchenko (1895–1958) was the talented author of numerous amusing satires on contemporary life in the early years of the Soviet regime. He mainly wrote short stories in a style known as "skaz"—the language of colloquial speech, as opposed to the higher style of literature—using it to comment on the frustrations of everyday life. His work had the effect of denying the importance of the imperatives of Soviet ideology by focusing on the day-to-day petty trials faced by his protagonists: in effect, he made fun of everything, from the ideology he purposely omitted from his prose to trivialities such as broken boots that he described in almost ludicrous detail.

Zoshchenko, who was born in Poltava, first came to study at St. Petersburg University law school in 1913. He lived in this apartment, home now to the museum, from 1934–58, except during the Second World War, when he was evacuated to Alma Ata. The museum is not easy to find, but it is undoubtedly worth persevering to visit this hidden memorial to the writer. Take a right on the corner of No. 4 Ulitsa Malaia Konniushennaia nearest to Nevskii Prospect, and then the first left into the courtyard, and the entrance is on the left. A small plaque by the door is the only reference to the museum's existence. The museum evokes a unique sense of the creativity it once housed: it has an abundant display of memorabilia, including photographs, editions of Zoshchenko's work, and newspapers hanging from the walls and ceiling. Leading on from this main room is the writer's bedroom, in which stands a single bed, armoire, and bedside table, as well as his writing desk and his much-used typewriter

# Anna Akhmatova Memorial Museum
## Мемориальный музей Анны Ахматовой
## Memorial' nii muzei Anni Akhmatovoi

**24**

**Address:** 53 Liteinii Prospect,
St. Petersburg 199034
**Tel:** 272-2034 / 272-2211
**Website:** www.museum.ru/museum/akhmatova/
fountain_house

**Open:** 10:30A.M.–6:30 P.M.; closed Mondays
and the last Wednesday of very month
**Metro:** Dostoevskaia, Vladimirskaia, Maiakovskaia.
**Kiosk, lecture/cinema hall, public library,
café/bar, theater**

Ravishingly beautiful, with a tall, perfect figure to match; Anna Akhmatova (1889–1966), the most distinguished of Russian female poets, was the embodiment of the bohemian spirit of the early 20th century before the onset of the horrors of the First World War. A friend of Gor'kii, the poet Mandel'shtam, and Amedeo Modigliani, who painted the famous, striking portrait of her that once hung in the museum (now in a private collection), Akhmatova surrounded herself with numerous lovers, admirers, and friends. Married three times, she lived here in Fountain House for over 30 years, first arriving in 1918 with her second husband, the archaeologist and minor poet Vladimir Shileiko.

Until the Revolution, this beautiful 18th-century palace was the residence of the Sheremetev family. It was then handed over to the state and turned into communal apartments. Akhmatova lived here from 1926 to 1952 with her third husband, the art historian Nikolai Punin. Their third-floor apartment is now the location of the main Akhmatova Museum in Russia (along with the Museum of Musical Instruments; see pp. 64–65). It opened in June 1989, marking the centenary of her birth.

The years that Akhmatova spent in this house were for the most part bleak ones. Her first husband, the poet Nikolai Gumilev, was executed in St. Petersburg in 1921, and her son Lev Gumilev was arrested numerous times during the time of Stalin's purges. She always

*Sheremetev Palace*

*Painting of Akhmatova by Nathan Altman, 1914 in the State Russian Museum, St. Petersburg*

believed that the cause of his arrest was her meeting with Isaiah Berlin (the First Secretary of the British Embassy in Moscow in 1945), accused of being an "English spy." Despite the renown she had acquired with her first collection of verse, after the Revolution her poetry was condemned as unacceptable by the new regime. In 1946, the Communist Party branded her an "enemy of the people" and kept her under constant surveillance.

The museum consists of six rooms, which document different stages in Akhmatova's life and work. The first examines her life until 1920, her childhood at Tsarskoe Selo (also known as Pushkin, it is south of St. Petersburg), her early adulthood in St. Petersburg, and her first publications. With the aid of manuscripts, rare editions, posters, photographs, and portraits, the museum documents Akhmatova's life during the Revolution (room 2) and throughout the 1930s (room 4). The third room, where she lived until 1938, still contains the white ceramic stove and several other pieces of original furniture, including a red sofa, Punin's desk, a bookcase, a table, and some of her personal belongings. After the breakup of her marriage to Punin, she moved into the room that had previously been inhabited by Punin's first wife. On display are books from her library donated to the museum by Punin's family, her writing desk, little known portraits and photographs of Akhmatova and her contemporaries, an icon, a mirror, and a candlestick. A chair, a chaise longue, and a small table complete the sparsely furnished room. The "House on the Fontanka" features in many of Akhmatova's poems, and even today it manages to conjure up the austere but dazzlingly creative life story of one of Russia's greatest artists.

On the second floor of the building is a concert and exhibition hall, where literary and musical soirees are held by Russian and foreign artists. On the ground floor there is a video-room café, where visitors can watch films about 20th-century Russian poets.

N.B. There are two other museums dedicated to Akhmatova in the town of Pushkin.

# Museum of the Defense and the Blockade of Leningrad

Музей обороны и блокады Ленинграда

## Muzei oboroni i blokadi Leningrada

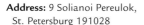

**Address:** 9 Solianoi Pereulok,
St. Petersburg 191028
**Tel:** 275-7115 / 275-7208 / 279-3021
**Website:** www.museum.ru/M107
**Open:** 10 A.M.–4 P.M. daily, except
Tuesdays 10 A.M.–5 P.M.

**Metro:** Chernishchevskaia
**Further directions:** Bus 46 runs from Ulitsa
Kirochnaia to the corner of Ulitsa Pestel' and
Solianoi Pereulok
**Kiosk/shop**

The devastating siege of Leningrad lasted 900 days, from September 8, 1941, to January 27, 1944; estimates of the number of people who died range from 164,000 to 800,000. Despite the horrific bombing and shelling of the city, starvation due to diminishing food supplies, and the agony of three Russian winters in these conditions, the citizens of Leningrad refused to surrender to the German troops and battled on valiantly, attempting to keep the city's industrial and cultural lives aglow. As a result, the siege of Leningrad gained international significance, and its victims will always be admired the world over. Although a museum cannot do full justice to the immense bravery of the city's victims, this Museum of the Blockade nevertheless provides a descriptive and evocative account of the horrors the city underwent.

The museum building was built in 1901–03 in the area then known as Solianii Gorodok (lit-

erally "little salt town," because it had many warehouses storing salt and wine reserves). It originally housed the Kustarnii Museum with displays on rural industries, but was turned into the Museum of Defense and the Blockade of Leningrad in January 1946. Fortunes changed in 1953 owing to the so-called "Leningrad Affair," a time following the end of the Second World War

*Main entrance to the Blockade Museum*

*Selection of Russian army helmets*

Hung on the opposite wall is a large collection of photographs of the archaeologists working to uncover remnants of the blockade. In the center of the hall stands a reconstruction of a typical building in the blockade, showing what living conditions would have been like at that time.

The farthest end of the hall is, however, by far the most evocative part of the exhibit, giving visitors a sense of just how horrendous conditions were. Here there are articles from German and Russian newspapers describing the events; information about the workers and schoolchildren who attempted to carry on with their daily routine during the blockade; and a large reproduction of a painting by Savinov, showing the city lit up by gunfire and bombs and the inhabitants running for shelter. A display case contains three German army uniforms over which symbolically hangs a wooden cross. The most heart-rending exhibits are the drawings and descriptions by the children of Leningrad. A sixteen-year-old boy described the meal he wished to eat after the blockade—a day he was destined not to see —and a ten-year-old boy's diary entry tells of the soup his mother made from some leftover glue and the gradual wasting away of his bedridden father. A visitor to this museum cannot escape a feeling of innermost horror on reading these accounts, and cannot fail to be moved by the numerous documents testifying to the courage of those whose names should forever be inscribed into the tormented history of this heroic city.

when Leningrad began to thrive and Stalin became weary of its increasing autonomy and the popularity of its blockade heroes. Wanting to repress the triumphal surge of the city, Stalin arrested many of the city's leading figures, including A. A. Kuznetsov, P. S. Popov, and Y. F. Lazutin, and had them shot. As a result, most of the museum's huge stock of exhibits were either given away or destroyed. However, owing to strong public demand, the museum was reopened in 1989.

The museum now holds over 35,000 items, many of which have been donated by the survivors of the blockade and their families. The first half of the exhibit contains clothing and uniforms worn by the inhabitants and workers of the city and those serving in the Red Army.

**63**

# Museum of Musical Instruments
## Sheremetev Palace (Fountain House)
Музей музыкальных инструментов
Шереметевский дворец (Фонтанный Дом)
### Muzei muzikal'nikh instrumentov
**Sheremetevskii dvorets (Fontannii Dom)**
**A branch of the Museum of Theatrical and Musical Arts**

**26**

**Address:** 34 Naberezhnaia reki Fontanki,
  St. Petersburg 190104
**Tel:** 272-2123 / 272-5818 / 272-5939
**Website:** www.museum.ru/M102
**Open:** 12 P.M.–6 P.M., Wednesday to Sunday

**Metro:** Gostinii Dvor, Nevskii Prospect, Maiakovskaia
**Further directions:** Buses 3, 7, 22, and 27 and
  trolleybuses 1, 5, 7, 10, and 22 run from the
  metros to the bridge on Nevskii Prospect over the
  Fontanka.

It's hard to believe that just around the corner from the busy Nevskii Prospect on the Fontanka River is the stunning former palace of the Sheremetevs, once the biggest landowning family in the world. It became a focal point for St. Petersburg's operatic and musical life. The Sheremetevs' theatrical troupe was made up of serfs trained as singers and performers, and was the most important of its kind in its day, attracting many prominent visitors.

The palace was built on marshland given by Peter the Great in 1712 to Boris Sheremetev, field marshal of his army at the Battle of Poltava. As part of his plan for the city, and his wish to westernize the Russian aristocracy, the tsar asked that a European-style palace be built on the land. After Boris died in 1719, Peter took his sole surviving son, Piotr, under his wing and brought him up at court. His connections made him not only a favorite of Catherine the Great, but also brought the family great wealth in the form of land and serfs granted in reward for their services. Marriage aided the process when Piotr married a wealthy heiress, adding the estate of Ostankino, outside Moscow, to their holdings. Much of their wealth went on constructing lavish palaces, holding balls, buying extravagant clothes, and keeping their enormous household staffs (there were 340 servants at Sheremetev Palace). Their son Nikolai Petrovich became the estate's third owner. He inherited his father's love for music and opera. Music and opera were the soul of the palace; the performances both here and at their other estate at Kuskovo attracted even the Empress Catherine. As the performances at the palace became legendary, so did Nikolai's romance with the beautiful serf Praskovia. A soprano of note, she became a legend in her own right. He later married her in

*The Antique Reception Room*

secret and she gave birth a year later, only to die several weeks later from complications. On her death, Nikolai succeeded in having their son, Dmitri, recognized as the sole legitimate heir to his great fortune.

Originally constructed from wood, Fountain House was later rebuilt in stone by Piotr. It is a good example of the synthesis of Italian and Russian baroque styles that you can still see in the city, perfected by the Italian architect B. Rastrelli. It is believed that he may have designed the house, certainly his assistant Savva Chevakinskii played a part in its construction. Its classical façade is adorned with the family crest decorated with lions holding palm branches, as are the ornate iron fences and gates that surround the palace. The last private owner of Fountain House, Sergei Sheremetev, handed the palace and its collections to the state in 1918. During Soviet times it suffered, and much of the original decoration (including French wallpaper, used for the first time in Russia here) was lost. Later it was used to house a number of museum collections and today contains a memorial museum in the south garden wing, which was at one time the home of the Russian poet Anna Akhmatova (see pp. 60-61).

Today, part of the stunning private collection of the Sheremetev family is on view, while works by Raphael, Correggio, Rembrandt, and others, which once graced the walls are now hanging in the Hermitage of the Winter Palace. In the second-floor reception rooms, restored in the late 1980s, there are selected sculptures, paintings of family members, porcelain collections, silver, weaponry, coins, icons (originally from the palace's church), books, and the family's archives. Since 1997 the palace's gallery wing on the ground floor has formed a stunning backdrop to a selection of instruments from a collection numbering over 3,000. The core originates from the head of the Court Orchestra, Baron Konstantin Shtakelberg (1848-1925). There are also holdings from the former Leningrad Institute of Theater, Music, and Cinematography. Display cases are crammed full: there are violins by Stradivarius and Amati; a set of horns that formed an orchestra; several hundred flutes; folk and ethnographic instruments, including Chinese gongs; and instruments once owned by the composers Mikhail Glinka (1804-57), Piotr Chaikovskii (1840-93), and Anton Rubenstein (1829-94). Upstairs a whole room is devoted to their collection of spinets and harpsichords, including a very early Italian spinet from 1532. Musical performances are held regularly in White Hall, off the second floor.

**65**

# N. A. Nekrasov Apartment-Museum
Музей-квартира Н. А. Некрасова
## Muzei-kvartira N. A. Nekrasova
**A branch of the All-Russian A. S. Pushkin Museum**

**27**

**Address:** 36 Liteinii Prospect,
   St. Petersburg 191104
**Tel:** 272-0165 / 272-0481
**Website:** www.museumpushkin.ru

**Open:** 11 A.M.–5 P.M.; closed Tuesdays and
   the last Friday of every month.
**Metro:** Chernishchevskaia

*Who Is Happy in Russia?* (*Komu na Rusi zhit'
khorosho?*) was the title of one of Nekrasov's
many polemical poems that established him as
a powerful and talented satirical writer. Such
lines from his poetic attacks on Russia were
widely used by revolutionaries, who, like
Nekrasov himself, were bent on improving
social conditions in the country. Nekrasov was
born in Moscow in 1821 to a Russian father
and Polish mother. His combined love of poetry and sensitivity to the fate of the Russian
peasantry brought his poetic talents to
fruition at the age of seven. However, much of
his early life was spent in abject poverty
because his merciless father rejected him for
having entered university. While working as a
critic for the journal *Notes of the Fatherland*
(*Otechestvennie zapiski*), he was taken under the
wing of the well-known critic Vissarion
Belinskii and was thus given the opportunity
to pursue his fascination with social and political contemporary thought. What followed was
an illustrious career as a publisher, editor, and

*Portrait of Nekrasov (1872) by Nikolai Gay*

It was in this flat on Liteinii Prospect that Nekrasov spent the last 20 years of his life, and where he worked as editor-in-chief in the offices of *The Contemporary*. (These offices were in the same building.) The success and popularity of the journal meant that equally famous members of St. Petersburg's literary circles such as Ivan Turgenev, Nikolai Chernishchevskii, Mikhail Saltikov-Shchedrin, and Leo Tolstoi often visited this building.

The museum, established in 1946, focuses on aspects of literary life after the death of Pushkin, and on Nekrasov's life and work. The collection contains many of Nekrasov's personal belongings, editions of the journals that he worked on, and many portraits of the writer and his contemporaries (including those of his mistress and literary collaborator, Avdotia Panaeva). Recently, "Panaev's quarters" were opened up to visitors. Here the visitor can see the study of Ivan Panaev, Nekrasov's friend and colleague, as well as a display dedicated to the development of journalism in Russia from the 1830s to the 1860s. Those interested in any aspect of the history of Russian literary life and work will find this museum worth a visit. It serves as a fascinating complement to and continuation of the other exhibits in the All-Russian A. S. Pushkin Museum.

Please note that a new exhibition is due to open in 2003 at 118 Naberezhnaia reki Fontanki, dedicated to the poet Gavrila Derzhavin and also under the auspices of the All-Russian A. S. Pushkin Museum.

*Nikolai Nekrasov in the period of* Last Songs *(1877–78) by Ivan Kramskoi*

writer, which, surprisingly, fared well despite the problems of censorship at the time. He is most famed for his work on the journal *The Contemporary* (*Sovremennik*) and for his writing, which conveys a sense of Russian peasant diction. On his death in 1878, Dostoevskii eulogized about him, comparing him to Russia's great writers Pushkin and Lermontov.

# Smol'nii Museum
Смольный музей
**Smol'nii muzei**

28

**Address:** Kom. 137, 3 Smol'nii, Ploshchad'
  Proletarskoi Diktaturi, St. Petersburg 193060
**Tel:** 276-1461
**Website:** www.museum.ru/M109
**Open:** 10 A.M.–5 P.M., Monday to Friday

**Metro:** Chernishchevskaia
**Further directions:** Bus 22 runs from the metro
  to Smol'nii or take trolleybus 49 as far as it
  goes along Suvorovskii Prospect.

This magnificent Classical building by the Italian architect Giacomo Quarenghi was originally commissioned in 1806 by Maria Feodorovna, wife of Paul I, as an institution to educate the female offspring of the nobility to who went on to serve in the imperial court. The events of 1917 saw the role of the Smol'nii Institute (named after the area, known as Smolianoi Dvor, where they tarred the ships during the time of Peter the Great) alter dramatically. It became the Bolshevik headquarters and the heart of the great Revolution. Besides the Bolshevik Central Committee it housed all the great revolutionary institutions, including the Military-Revolutionary Committee, *Sovnarkom* (Soviet People's Committee), and the Petrograd Soviet. From November of that year, Vladimir Lenin and his wife, Nadezhda Krupskaia, moved into a two-room apartment on the second floor. Lenin's office was room no. 81 on the third floor, and opposite was his reception room, where he met with visitors. Trotskii and his family lived opposite them, and there was a communal cafeteria. The halls and meeting rooms were full of colleagues and representatives from the other revolutionary bodies. Lenin was surrounded by revolutionary politics and found it very comforting. He stayed until March the following year, when he and the Central Committee moved to Moscow.

The building went on to serve political bodies, housing the first Soviet government and the various committees of the Communist Party until 1991. Lenin's apartment was transformed into a museum in 1927, and in 1974 his study was also opened to visitors. The spartan living room where Lenin and his wife lived, with a screen separating the living area from the bed, survives with much of its original furnishings, as does Lenin's study. Many of their personal belongings remain, and displays of documents record the revolutionary events of 1917–18.

*Exterior of the Smol'nii Institute*

# Suvorov Museum
## Музей А. В. Суворова
### Muzei A. V. Suvorova

**29**

**Address:** 43 Ulitsa Kirochnaia,
  St. Petersburg 193015
**Tel:** 279-3914
**Website:** www.museum.ru/M108
**Open:** 10 A.M.–6 P.M., Thursday to Monday;
  closed the first Monday of every month

**Metro:** Chernishchevskaia
**Further directions:** Bus 22 and trolleybus 49 run
  from the metro to the museum
**Kiosk/shop, lecture/cinema hall**

This museum is devoted to one of Russia's most outstanding generals, Alexander Vasilievich Suvorov (1729–1800). He was an able military strategist and commander who achieved his greatest glory during the reigns of Catherine the Great and Paul I. Despite his toughness and lack of concern for the lives of his men, Suvorov's eccentric personality (he used to perform naked somersaults in front of his army every morning) won him the love of his troops, crucial for achieving military successes against the odds. He won at Kinburn against the Ottoman forces despite being wounded twice. He believed in charging regardless of the consequences (his greatest battles at Ismail and Praga were bloodbaths), and on several occasions was able to defeat the most prominent generals in the French Revolutionary Wars of 1798–99, despite having to cross the Alps in the most appalling conditions. One of Prince Grigori Potemkin's (1739–91) supreme generals, he spoke six foreign languages and was knowl-edgeable in ancient history and literature. Despite his illustrious career, which earned him numerous titles and orders, Suvorov's death was not duly commemorated. He returned to St. Petersburg in disgrace following a series of

*Portrait of Suvorov*

*Exterior of the Suvorov Museum*

defeats and retreats in the Alps. Paul I was unsympathetic to his pleas for a hearing on the attacks his army had endured. He died from exhaustion and illness in St. Petersburg and lies buried in the Aleksandr Nevskii Monastery (see pp. 82-83). He is honored by a plaque laid within a year of his death by Aleksandr I in the Field of Mars.

The museum first opened in 1900 to commemorate the centenary of Suvorov's death. Four years later it moved to this specially designed museum, built with donations from civilians and the military. It was designed by the architect A. von Gogen in the style of an old Russian fortress, complete with a watchtower decorated with the Count's coat of arms. The wings of the building are adorned with mosaics by N. Maslennikov and M. Zoshchenko (father of the writer Mikhail Zoshchenko). One features Suvorov as he departs from his family estate,

Konchanskii village, for the Italian campaign in 1799; the other depicts him leading his troops over the Alps after a picture by Aleksei Popov. During the First World War the building was bombed heavily. However, with the approaching German troops in sight, its contents were evacuated to Siberia for safekeeping. After the war they were restored to the museum, but it was not long before the collection was closed again and the building became a club. Stalin ordered it open in 1950, but as a military museum rather than a memorial. It was not until the late 1980s that it regained its former status.

The collection contains over 110,000 items. Most notable are Suvorov's personal belongings such as his awards, weapons (the bayonet was his favorite), banners, uniforms, autographs, and books. Hung throughout the exhibition space are some of the many portraits of the general, and there are several large panoramas recreating historic battlefields. A considerable number of objects have been donated by various people, including V. Engelgard, who went to Europe and amassed wagonloads of memorabilia, most of it connected with the Swiss campaign of 1799. One of Suvorov's descendants, the last owner of the family estate, donated some of his orders and even his plumes. From Tsar Nikolai II came many of the Count's documents. Besides this array of memorabilia the museum displays some 60,000 Russian and European miniature soldiers, one of the largest exhibits of its type in the country.

**71**

# Bread Museum
## Музей хлеба
### Muzei khleba

**Address:** 73 Ligovskii Prospect,
  St. Petersburg 191040
**Tel:** 164-1110
**Website:** www.museum.ru/museum/bread

**Open:** 10 A.M.–5 P.M., Tuesday to Saturday;
  closed the last Tuesday of every month
**Metro:** Ligovskii Prospect
**Kiosk/shop**

The history of bread and the history of humankind are inextricably linked. In Russian culture, bread is perhaps even more significant than in the West. It was never just food; instead, it played an iconic part in Russian popular culture, with religious and symbolic importance. Peasant rituals of all kinds used bread in endless forms, from loaves shaped like ladders placed next to the dead in their graves to assist them on the way to heaven, to bread shaped like birds baked in the spring to mark the return of migratory flocks. Bread was given as gifts, offered to visitors, used to greet a newborn child, had hymns and songs written about it, was frequently mentioned in Russian literature, and remains a main part of the Russian diet. It seems, then, bread certainly deserves to have a museum devoted to it.

Tucked away behind the Moscow Station on the premises of the Bread Bakery Plant is this hidden gem. A tiny elevator takes visitors to the fourth floor, where an English-speaking guide offers visitors a wide range of bread-related merchandise before beginning the

*Soviet-style bedroom from the time of the Blockade*

*A 19th-century kitchen*

tour. The size of this museum belies its scope: two of its four rooms house a comprehensive collection of breadmaking apparatus, which visitors are encouraged to pick up and touch, along with pictures documenting the history of breadmaking in Russia. Exhibits show the baking activities of different civilizations, from the Stone Age to the ancient Egyptians and from Russian medieval bakers right up to modern techniques of bread production.

The third room is devoted to the role of bread in Russian literature. One showcase documents Pushkin's references to bread in his works, and even suggests what food the writer might have eaten while composing them. The fourth room contains an exhibit on the siege of Leningrad. The visitor is introduced to the various improvised bread substitutes that were the staple diet of St. Petersburg's wartime inhabitants. Particularly striking is the selection of industrial breadmaking machines used during Soviet times, above which are hung Soviet banners and flags. Small but perfectly formed, the museum is a unique and intriguing find.

*Soviet industrial bread ovens*

**73**

# F. M. Dostoevskii Literary Memorial Museum

Литературно-мемориальный музей Ф. М. Достоевского

## Literaturno-memorial'nii muzei F. M. Dostoevskogo

**31**

**Address:** 5/2 Kuznechnii Pereulok,
 St. Petersburg 654034
**Tel:** 311-4031 / 311-1804
**Website:** www.md.spb.ru

**Open:** 11 A.M.– 5:30 P.M.; closed Mondays
 and the last Wednesday of every month
**Metro:** Vladimirskaia, Dostoevskaia
**Kiosk/shop, lecture/cinema hall**

The museum is housed in the basement and on two floors of the building where Dostoevskii spent the last three years of his life (1878–81). Whenever he rented an apartment in St. Petersburg, it was located so that at least one window had a view of a church—in this case it is the Vladimirskaia Church. The apartment consists of seven rooms, each arranged to reflect its appearance when the writer and his wife, Anna Grigorievna, and his two children, Liubov' and Fiodor, lived here. Archival plans, drawings, and memoirs of the writer's contemporaries were used for the reconstruction, with his study arranged according to a photograph made after his death. The apartment reflects a stable period in his life, when Dostoevskii, tired of gambling, lived as a quiet family man and worked on what is perhaps the greatest of his novels, *The Brothers Karamazov.*

 The museum contains both the apartment and a literary exhibit describing his career as a writer and the novels for which he is most

*Interior of Dostoevskii
Literary Memorial Museum*

famous. The apartment itself was reconstructed using photographs kept in the museum's archives. On display here are many of the writer's old possessions, many of which have been donated to the museum by his descendants. There is a vast collection of documents and photographs describing his life and work, as well as a collection of graphic and applied art and some of the writer's old manuscripts. The museum's library holds about 24,000 volumes and a selection of theater posters and programs from various performances of Dostoevskii's plays.

The literary display is laid out in chronological order, showing the various stages in his career. The beginning describes his imprisonment and impending death sentence, which was revoked at the last minute. Instead he was exiled to Tobolsk in Siberia for a period of four years (1850–54). The notion of awaiting one's own death haunted the writer and was discussed in depth in many of his novels, in particular in *The Idiot*. The remainder of the display section is dedicated to his major novels, with one display case for each novel, containing some of the most significant aspects from each of these works.

This museum is definitely worth a visit, even for those with little or no knowledge of either Dostoevskii or Russian literature. Small guides are available inside the museum, written in a variety of languages, including Russian, English, and French, to help visitors find their way around the museum and learn more about one of Russia's greatest writers and philosophical thinkers.

# October Railway Central Museum
Центральный музей Октябрьской железной дороги

## Tsentral'nii muzei Oktiabr'skaia zheleznoi dorogi

32

**Address:** 114 Obvodnii Kanal Embankment,
  St. Petersburg 198052
**Tel:** 168-2629

**Open:** 11 A.M.–5 P.M., Monday to Friday
**Metro:** Frunzenskaia, Baltiiskaia

## & The Museum of Railway Equipment at the Warsaw Railway Terminal
Музей железнодожной техники на Варшавском вокзале

## Muzei zheleznodorozhnoi tekhniki na Varshavskom vokzale

**Address:** 118 Obvodnii Kanal Embankment,
  St. Petersburg 198147
**Tel:** 168-2063
Tours and a leaflet are available in English

**Open:** daily 11 A.M.–5 P.M. from May 1 to Nov. 1;
  11 A.M.–5 P.M , Wednesday to Sunday,
  Nov. 2–April 30
**Metro:** Frunzenskaia, Baltiiskaia

When the Warsaw railway terminal closed to rail traffic in 2001 it was only months before it was transformed into this new museum for the core collections of the Oktiabr'skaia (October) Railway. This museum is for railway enthusiasts who prefer to see full-size engines, carriages, and related railway paraphernalia. Those who are more interested in seeing models should visit the Central Museum of Railway Transport (see pp. 45-46).

This collection, started in 1991, was previously on display in the railway station in Shushari. It tells the history of Russian railways, which began on October 30, 1837, when the first steam engine traveled between St. Petersburg and Tsarskoe Selo, one of the suburban summer residences of the tsars. It was not until 1851 that regular rail traffic linked St. Petersburg and Moscow. Today, Oktiabr'skaia Railway services a population exceeding 25 million, with links to the European railway network. Railway devotees will not be disappointed: this collection is unique (there are still no railway museums in Moscow) and contains the best examples of historic railway engines and carriages in the country.

Containing over 50,000 items, this collection shows the development of the railway in northwestern Russia, comprising about 30 railway routes, from the early days to the present. The collection is displayed over two separate areas near the terminal. The collections of the **October Railway Museum**

*The S.68, one of the best passenger locomotives in Russia before the Revolution*

in one large exhibition room consist of original railway uniforms from the beginning of the 20th century up to the present day, models of engines, railway badges, documents, and numerous other items recounting the history of the railway.

The real gem, however, is **The Museum of Railway Equipment,** situated on the tracks of the railway terminal, which holds the impressive collection of restored engines, diesel locomotives, and a railway artillery system used in the 1930s and during the war. Displayed over more than a mile (1.5 km) of tracks in the open yard are only around half (approximately 80) of the engines and cars in the collection. The b2023 tank engine, built by the Kolomenskii Works in 1897 and used for shunting, opens the display. It is one of the oldest surviving locomotives in Russia. Nearby is the S.68, one of the best passenger locomotives built in Russia before the Revolution; it is the only survivor of its class. Designed by B. S. Malakhovskii, chief engineer of the Sormovo works (hence the class name S),

it was probably built by the Nevskii Works in Petrograd in 1917 (Petrograd was the name for St Petersburg from 1914-24, after which it was changed to Leningrad, 1924-41). It was steam locomotives of this class that transported the Soviet government officials from Petrograd to Moscow in March 1918, including, it is claimed, Lenin. It was preserved as a monument to Lenin and was to be placed at Leningradskii Station in Moscow, but when the political climate changed it was transferred to St. Petersburg. The diesel and electric locomotives on display denote the beginning of diesel engine building and electrification in the Soviet Union. The section containing railway equipment from the Second World War holds a TM-3-12 305mm rail-mounted gun. Plans are in place to cover this open area to help preserve this valuable collection.

Railway enthusiasts should contact the engineer at the museum, Sergei Pogodin, who by prior arrangement will take groups to the open marshaling yard (Sortirovachnaia Station) at Shushari, approximately half an hour by train or metro. Here visitors can see the original museum yard, where additional locomotives and carriages are kept and are being restored.

*The Ov 6640, used as an armored train in the Second World War*

77

# Rimskii-Korsakov Memorial Museum-Apartment

Мемориальный музей-квартира Н. А. Римского-Корсакова

## Memorial'nii muzei-kvartira N. A. Rimskogo-Korsakova

### A branch of the Museum of Theatrical and Musical Arts

**33**

**Address:** 28 Zagorodnii Prospect,
  St. Petersburg 191002
**Tel:** 113-3208 / 315-3975
**Website:** www.opera.r2.ru/rus

**Open:** 11 A.M.–6 P.M., Wednesday to Sunday;
  closed the last Friday of every month
**Metro:** Vladimirskaia, Dostoevskaia
**Further directions:** Trolleybuses 3, 8, and 15
  run from the metro to the museum

It was in this apartment that the great composer Nikolai Rimskii-Korsakov (1844–1908) lived for the last 15 years of his life. Having risen to become part of the Russian musical establishment, including becoming professor at the St. Petersburg Conservatory, it was here he wrote 11 of his 15 operas, including *Sadko*, *The Tsar's Bride*, and *The Golden Cockerel,* as well as his autobiography, *The Story of My Musical Life*. It became one of the hubs of St. Petersburg's musical and artistic life, with regular parties and weekly meetings of such composers as Rakhmaninov, Stravinskii, and Scriabin, as well as singers and artists.

Born in a tiny town 125 miles (200 km) from St. Petersburg, Nikolai was destined from a young age to become a composer, but it was not a straightforward path. Although he could play the piano well, his parents thought of his music as "foolish" and enrolled him in the Naval School at St. Petersburg when he was 12.

But their plan backfired, and during this time he was able to attend the best operas and concerts of the day, fueling his love of music. Encouragement came from as new teacher, who taught him the rules of composition and urged him to try composing. His parents interfered again and insisted he become a naval officer, which meant sailing around the world. There were no instruments aboard ship, let alone time for music, and his passion waned. Upon his return he gave up hope of continuing his music, until he met up with his musical friends, who encouraged him to complete his symphony in 1865. Hailed as a great success, his career was launched.

Four rooms, including the study, living room, dining room, and entrance hall, were authentically restored and opened as a memorial museum in 1971. A large number of the composer and his family's personal effects are displayed in these rooms and in the exhibition

*Rimskii-Korsakov's piano*

hall. Upon his death, his widow, Nadezhda Nikolaievna, made a list of items she thought might be used in a museum commemorating her husband. His descendants presented 250 of these to the museum, including his precious grand piano (also played by many of his friends), musical scripts, playbills of performances, family portraits (all the way back to his great-great-grandmother), and his wife's writing desk. Beautiful period furniture fills the rooms, and his fur coat still hangs by the former entrance, along with a selection of visiting cards of other musicians.

In addition, there is a small concert hall with 50 seats, where recitals and concerts are held several times a week. Check with the museum for dates and times.

**79**

# Museum of the Arctic and Antarctic
## Музей Арктики и Антарктики
### Muzei Arktiki i Antarktiki

**34**

**Address:** 24-a Ulitsa Marata,
St. Petersburg 191040
**Tel:** 113-1998
**Website:** www.polarmuseum.sp.ru

**Open:** 10 A.M.–5 P.M., Wednesday to Sunday
**Metro:** Vladimirskaia, Dostoevskaia, Maiakovskaia,
Ploshchad' Vosstania
**Kiosk/shop, lecture/cinema hall**

Built in 1838, the Church of St. Nicholas the Miracle Worker, designed by Abraham Ivanovich Melnikov, has been cleverly modified to accommodate this world-class museum devoted to the discovery and history of exploration, the natural environment, economy, and culture of the polar regions. Thousands of exhibits dating back to the 16th century are set out around four major themes: the Arctic, the discovery and history of exploration of the Northern Sea Route, the economy and culture of the northern regions, and Antarctica.

Besides featuring the flora, fauna, and geography of the Arctic in splendid dioramas, the first section focuses on the glories of the Russian explorers in the region from the 11th century up to recent times. It was the daring voyages of Russians who lived along the White Sea coast that gave the world some of the first Arctic discoveries. Later, under Peter the Great, the Russian Imperial Navy mapped extensive areas and made significant discoveries.

There are artifacts, models, and maps relating to pioneers of Arctic and Antarctic exploration such as Semen Dezhnev (1605/08–72), the Cossack navigator who in 1648 made the first recorded voyage through the Bering Strait; Vitus Bering, who led the Great Northern Expedition (1733–45) that discovered the Aleutians and Komandorskie Islands; Admiral Makarov on the first-ever icebreaker "Ermak" (1900–01); and the historic Antarctic expedition under F. Bellinsgausen

*Exterior of the museum*

and maps, there is a hall devoted to the indigenous peoples of the northern regions, containing exhibits of natural resources, traditional clothing made of reindeer fur, ivory carvings, and artifacts of the native peoples of Siberia.

The Polar Philatelic Collection is outstanding and contains some of the best examples of polar philately anywhere, commemorating the work of explorers and scientists from Russia and abroad who ventured forth into the Arctic and Antarctic. Equally exceptional is the numismatic collection of over 4,000 pieces, including coins dating back to the 16th and 17th centuries as well as medals awarded to polar explorers and pilots.

*Relief map of the Arctic*

and M. Lazarev, which included the brilliant astronomer I. Simonov. Peering into the windows of the black leather tent marked in white with "CCCP" on one side and "North Pole-1" on the other, visitors can see bunk beds covered with fur, a radio station, and bookshelves. This is the legendary tent established on a drifting ice floe in the 1937-38 Soviet North Pole expedition led by Ivan Papanin.

Besides displays of models of expedition vessels, reports, charts, original equipment,

*Warm, protective clothing worn in the Antarctic*

**81**

# State Museum of Urban Sculpture
Государственный музей городской скульптуры
**Gosudarstvennii muzei gorodskoi skul'pturi**

## 35

**Address:** 179/2a Nevskii Prospect,
St. Petersburg 193167
**Tel:** 277-1716 / 325-9835 / 595-4133

**Website:** www.museum.ru/M111
**Open:** 10 A.M.–6 P.M.; closed Thursdays
**Metro:** Ploschad' Aleksandra Nevskogo

## *Branches*:
### Literatorskie Mostki
**Address:** 30 Rasstannaia Ulitsa,
St. Petersburg 192007
**Tel:** 166-2383
**Metro:** Ligovskii prospect
**Further directions:** Trams 10, 25, 44, and 49
run from the metro to Rasstannaia Ulitsa

### Narvskie Vorota
**Address:** 1 Ploshchad' Stachek,
St. Petersburg 198020
**Tel:** 186-9782
**Metro:** Narvskaia

St. Petersburg, the "Venice of the North," gained its reputation as one of the most fascinating and beautiful cities in the world because of its staggering wealth of monumental, architectural, and sculptural art. The city contains an overwhelming 3,700 monuments of federal importance, 2,300 of local importance, and more than 260 museums. The museum of urban sculpture, as the sole institution dealing with the restoration and preservation of Russian sculptures and monuments, purports to be one of the most frequently visited museums in the world. This is true given that it is responsible for more than 200 monuments and 1,500 memorial plaques in this city alone, including the Bronze Horseman, the Rostral Columns outside the Central Naval Museum, monuments around the city to the great rulers and figures of Russian history, and the Aleksandr Column in Winter Palace Square.

The main branch of the museum is located at the Aleksandr Nevskii Lavra (monastery). Peter I commissioned the monastery to be built in memory of Prince Aleksandr Nevskii. The site is open to visitors and is also used as the main center for the restoration work that the museum undertakes. Visitors can wander around the 18th-century Necropolis, the Arts Masters'

*Grave of a Russian nobleman, 19th century*

Necropolis (Lazarev and Tikhvin Cemeteries), and the Church of the Annunciation. The latter is the only church in St. Petersburg to remain unaltered since the time of Peter I. Together, the church and cemeteries hold a wealth of sculptures and tombstones belonging to some of the greatest names of Russia's history. Some of the most notable gravestones that can be seen here belong to the writer and scientist M. V. Lomonosov; the novelists N. M. Karamzin and F. M. Dostoevskii; the composers M. I. Glinka and P. I. Chaikovskii; and Field Marshal A. V. Suvorov. The headstones are veritable works of artistic genius, signifying the eminence of the people they commemorate. Sculptures in the process of being restored

cannot be viewed by the public until work on them is completed. Many of the monuments being restored have been brought to this center from the vast expanse of European and Asian Russia.

The museum has two further branches in the city: *Literatorskie Mostki*, the Necropolis museum of the Volkhov cemetery; and the Narvskie Gates. The former was originally a burial ground for poor people. However, it became the final resting place of a host of well-known Russian figures, such as the disgraced writer Aleksandr Radishchev; the famous 19th-century novelist and playwright Ivan Turgenev; and the 20th-century poet Aleksandr Blok. The Narvskie Gates, made of brick with a copper coating by the architect V. Stasov, were erected to celebrate the victories achieved by the Russian guards during the Patriotic War against Napoleon's army in 1812. These impressive gates dominate the view of Stachek Square, south of the city center. Inside the gate itself is a small accompanying museum, opened in 1987. It details the events of the war and has on display portraits of past military leaders, documents relating to the construction of the gates, and battle scenes.

In total, the museum holds 5,800 items in its collection, including 813 sculptures. It has a huge reserve of documents, including 2,611 negatives, 31,429 printed photographs, and 10,881 volumes of books. The museum is a splendid reminder of the magnificence and vastness of Russia's rich heritage of eminent ancestors.

**83**

# Branches of the All-Russian A. S. Pushkin Museum
# Lyceum Лицей Litsei

## 36

**Address:** 2 Sadovaia Ulitsa, Pushkin 189620

**Tel:** 812-476-6411

**Directions:** Train from Vitebskii Station to Detskoe Selo station (15.5 miles/25km; approx. 30 mins)

or bus 287 or 20 from Moskovskaia, then bus 371 or 382

**Open:** 10:30 A.M.–5:00 P.M.; closed Tuesdays and the last Friday of every month

# A. S. Pushkin Dacha-Museum
# (A. S. Pushkin Country House Museum)
## Музей-дача А.С. Пушкина Muzei-dacha A. S. Pushkina

**Address:** 2 Pushkinskaia Ulitsa, Pushkin 189620

**Directions:** Train from Vitebskii Station to Detskoe Selo station (15.5 miles/25km; approx. 30 mins)

or bus 287 or 20 from Moskovskaia, then bus 371

**Open:** Call the Lyceum Museum for opening times

These two branch museums are located in Pushkin (Tsarskoe Selo), a suburb of St. Petersburg located 15.5 miles (25 km) south of the city, named after the great writer in 1937 to commemorate the centenary of his death. As a student between 1811 and 1817, Pushkin studied at the **Lyceum**, the imperial school for boys from noble families. Under Emperor Aleksandr I, his adviser Mikhail Speranski set up this elite educational institution in 1811 modeled on the French school system. Aleksandr I commissioned the architect Vasilii Petrovich Stasov to refurbish a wing of the Catherine Palace in order to house the school. Its bold aims were to develop pupils' intellects in the hope that they would learn to think independently and later apply their talents in the service of the state. It was here that Pushkin realized his poetic genius and surrounded himself with devoted friends. His later works, including numerous poems and the novel *Eugene Onegin,* reflect the devotion Pushkin felt for his school and his appreciation for his outstanding education.

Opened in 1949 to mark the 150th anniversary of Pushkin's death, the entire building was refurbished over the next 25 years. Restored to its original layout using historic documents, rooms on the third and fourth floors where students spent most of

*Portrait of Pushkin by V. Tropinin,
original in the Pushkin Museum, Moscow*

their time have been opened as memorial rooms. The Great Hall, library, main staircase, and dormitories have also been restored. Materials on display include items associated with Pushkin's years here, along with his fellow pupils and the outstanding 18th-century poet Gavrila Derzhavin (1743–1816), who attended Pushkin's graduation ceremony in 1815 to, as Pushkin put it, "note and bless" him.

Special exhibits are arranged in some of the rooms, while others are host to musical evenings, meetings, and conferences. Every year, on October 19, the anniversary of the establishment of the Lyceum, an international festival is held, the Tsarskoe Selo Festival, when a program of art- and poetry-related events is held throughout the month in the museum and its surrounding gardens.

Pushkin's second visit to Tsarskoe Selo was in the summer of 1831. He and his wife, Natalia Goncharova, stayed at the country house of Anna Kitaeva, today known as the **Pushkin Dacha-Museum** (Pushkin Country House Museum). It's here that he worked for less than five months on one of his most famous works, *Eugene Onegin,* as well as his poem "Echo," and prepared his *Tales of Belkin* for publication. He enjoyed the peacefulness of his surroundings; after a swim in the morning at a nearby pond, followed by a cup of tea, he headed up to his study to begin work. Occupying 8 out of 11 rooms of the rented house, his study on the mezzanine floor was sparsely furnished but comfortable.

The dacha was opened as a museum in 1958, with new exhibitions added in 1981. Visitors can see Natalia's refurbished bedroom, Pushkin's study, displays of books, manuscripts, and personal possessions of Pushkin's friends, and other items related to the period. There are also two rooms dedicated to Pushkin's predecessors, the poet Vassilii Zhukovskii (1783–1852) and the writer and historian Nikolai Karamzin (1766–1826), both of whom had close links with Tsarskoe Selo.

**85**

# Tsarskoe Selo
## Царское Село

## 37

**Address:** 7 Ulitsa Sadovaia, Gorod Pushkin,
  Leningradakaia Oblast' 196600
**Tel:** 466-6674
**Website:** www.tsar.ru
**Open:** 10 A.M.–6 P.M.; closed Tuesdays and
  the last Monday of every month

**Directions:** Train from Vitebskii Station
(metro: Pushkinskaia) to Pushkin, (alternatively take
a private bus – minibus from metro Moskovskaia
to Pushkin), then bus 370, 371 or 378

The Tsars' Summer Residence in the small town of Pushkin, located 15.5 miles (25 km) south of St. Petersburg, is a unique and exquisite emblem of the extravagance and majesty of one of the world's most famous former autocracies. The site covers an area of just over 1,480 acres and contains an overwhelming 100 buildings. The architecture contained in the grounds of this palace exemplifies the artistic genius of some of the world's most famous architects, including Charles Cameron, Bartolomeo Rastrelli, and Giacomo Quarenghi, who designed the Aleksandr Palace to the north of the Great Palace.

This site was known as Saari Mois (meaning the "elevated land") until Peter the Great liberated the area from Swedish occupation. According to preserved maps, just one small manor house occupied the site. Peter first gave the land to his governor-general in charge of this area, Aleksandr Menshikov, before handing it over to his fiancée and future empress, Catherine. A small stone palace, known as "The Stone Chambers," was built here, and the site gradually

grew into a royal country residence with a small town built around it.

The first attempt to renovate the palace took place in 1742, during the reign of Empress Elizabeth I, according to a design by Mikhail Zemtsov. The work was not completed in Zemtsov's lifetime, instead the project was

*The Grand Palace*

*Cupolas on the Grand Palace*

dence by this extravagant yet mighty ruler. A particular example of this is the Cameron Gallery, built on the southwestern side of the Great Palace. Considered to be one of the most beautiful galleries in Europe, this was designed to be used by Catherine as a place for tranquil and philosophical contemplation.

The interiors of the palace are just as stunning and overwhelming as the numerous buildings scattered around the grounds. Visitors are invited to wander around the palace and take in the exquisite sumptuousness of the expansive apartments, which formerly belonged to Catherine the Great. Especially worth a visit are the Arabesque Room, the Chinese Drawing Rooms, the State Bedchamber, the Great Hall, and the Silver Study. The contrast in décor from room to room is astounding and exemplifies the precision and effort that went into making each of these apartments a unique masterpiece. Also noteworthy is the use of mirrors inside the palace—they enhance the sense of grandeur by creating the impression of an almost infinite expanse within the palace.

It is easy to spend a full day wandering around the palace and gardens, taking in the overwhelming splendor of the residence. The palace alone fascinates the visitor with its wealth and style, while a walk around the grounds, passing the grotto beside the lake, the Palladian Bridge, the Chinese Village, and the Aleksandr Palace, to name but a few, cannot fail to astound and impress.

overseen by a succession of architects, thus defeating the initial aim to create a unified palatial ensemble. As a result, on May 10, 1752, Elizabeth signed a decree commissioning Bartolomeo Rastrelli to undertake a complete overhaul of the palace. The residence thus gained its splendid blue, white, and gilt baroque façade and became a symbol of the wealth and grandeur of the Russian Empire.

A huge amount of work was similarly undertaken during the reign of Catherine the Great, renowned for her fascination with art and architecture and with the work of foreign architects, designers, and landscape gardeners. Several parts of the palace and its grounds reflect the personal stamp laid on the resi-

**87**

# Oranienbaum
## Ораниенбаум

**Address:** 48 Dvortsovii Prospect,
Lomonosov 189510
**Tel:** 422-4796 / 423-1641

**Open:** 10 A.M.–5 P.M.; closed Tuesdays
**Directions:** train from Baltiiskii Station
(metro: Baltiiskaia) to Oranienbaum

Foreigners rarely visit Oranienbaum, yet it contains three stunning 18th-century palaces—the Grand Place, the Palace of Peter III, and the Chinese Palace—as well as various smaller buildings of considerable interest. Situated 18 miles (29 km) due west of St. Petersburg along the road that passes the well-known palace complex of Peterhof, the estate sits facing the Gulf of Finland.

The history of Oranienbaum begins with the baroque Grand Place built in 1710–27 for Aleksandr Menshikov, who was appointed the first governor-general of St. Petersburg by Peter the Great. Contemporaries claimed its interiors were more impressive than those of the emperor's palaces; a sea canal was dug out to link the palace and its surrounding park with the Gulf of Finland. A regular French-style park was set out at the front of the palace, and the main body of the palace was linked by two long semi-circular galleries to two domed pavilions.

*The exterior of the Chinese Palace*

*The Sliding Hill Pavilion*

Menshikov soon after fell out of favor with Peter and the Great Palace stood languishing for 14 years. Despite being remodeled over the years, many of the original features have been retained, although most of the interior decoration was lost. Restoration in recent years has opened some of the rooms to the public, and visitors can also view the gardens.

In 1743 the Empress Elizabeth (daughter of Peter the Great) gave Oranienbaum to her nephew, the Grand Duke Peter Fedororvich, the future Emperor Peter III. Soon after, he was married to Catherine, the future Empress Catherine the Great. The Grand Duke's passion was playing with toy soldiers and model fortresses. He commissioned a toy military fortress to be built on the estate to indulge his obsession. Despite its miniature scale, the Peterstadt Fortress was built along the lines of an actual military fortress with five bastions, a moat, and fortifications. Besides a church, an arsenal, and guardhouse, a two-story stone building was added, the Palace of Peter III. Today, only the palace and a stone gate (the Gate of Honor) remain. While the interiors of the palace are not grand in scale, they are good examples of the early use of chinoiserie in Russia, with doors, panels, and door frames adorned with Chinese-style paintings. Centrally located in the palace is its Picture Hall, hung floor to ceiling with paintings by western European artists. While Peter continued enjoying his time on the estate, Catherine was plotting his demise. In 1762 the coup was implemented and Peter, after ruling for only one and a half years, was taken to Ropsha, not far from Oranienbaum, where he died several days later.

Just after Catherine came to the throne in 1762, she commissioned two of the most remarkable structures on the estate, the Chinese Palace and the Sliding Hill Pavilion (also known as the Switchback Pavilion). The architect chosen to design them was the brilliant Italian Antonio Rinaldi (who had also built Peterstadt Fortress and the Palace of Peter III). The elegant blue-and-white Sliding

**89**

*The Glass Bead Salon of the Chinese Palace*

Pavilion was built purely for play and pleasure. Originally, it had an undulating wooden ramp a third of a mile (0.5 km) long extending down from its second floor, on which sleds came down in the winter and carts in the summer. Sadly, this no longer exists, but the stunning interiors do remain, in particular the whimsical Porcelain Study. This is a room lined with swirling rococo decoration in keeping with the 40 Meissen figures of prancing horses and allegorical figures supported by leafy gilt-and-white consoles modeled by the porcelain factory's best designers, Kändler and Acier. Produced between 1772 and 1775, the room indulged Catherine's passion for porcelain and is invaluable for its historical significance.

There is, however, little doubt, that the real jewel at Oranienbaum is the marvelous Chinese Palace, considered one of the most beautiful of the suburban palaces outside St. Petersburg. It was Catherine's private dacha, where she entertained her friends and lovers during the "White Nights" (the days during the summer months when it stays light continuously). It was untouched during the German occupation, leaving intact dazzling rococo interiors considered among the best in Europe and unique in Russia. Rinaldi hired Italian painters and Russian craftsmen to create richly decorated and striking interiors that are truly breathtaking. The Grand Chinese Cabinet, which gave the palace its name, is lined with ivory- and wood-inlaid wall panels depicting scenes of an imaginary China, and the walls of the spectacular Glass Bead Salon are hung in panels of embroidered birds, flowers, and exotic landscapes set against a background of shimmering white glass beads.

Although the palace has survived its turbulent past, its defective drainage system and leaking roof are allowing water to seep back into the palace. Rising damp is breaking down the palace's plasterwork both inside and out and causing the parquet floors to buckle and pop. This unique structure is now clearly under threat from excess water. The World Monuments Fund in Britain has placed this work of art on its List of 100 Most Endangered Sites and begun raising funds to help ensure the preservation of this architectural gem.

# Kronstadt Fortress
Кронштадтская Крепость
## Kronshtadtskaia Krepost'

**39**

**Address:** 1 Yakornaia Square,
  St. Petersburg 189610
**Tel:** 236-4713 / 236-4450
**Website:** www.museum.navy.ru
**Open:** 11 A.M.–5:15 P.M., Wednesday to Sunday;
  closed the last Friday of every month
**Metro:** Chornaia Rechka

**Further directions:** Bus 510 or private bus
(minibus) K-510 from the metro to Kronstadt.
Alternatively, in the summer months, you can travel
to Oranienbaum from Baltiiskii train station and go
by boat ("The Meteor") from the Makarov
Embankment to Kronstadt.

This branch of the Central Navy Museum is based at Kronstradt, just 18 miles (29 km) outside St. Petersburg. The city and its fortress were built to protect St. Petersburg and the northwestern boundaries of Russia. The Russian Navy equipped its vessels here, and later, after a fire in St. Petersburg, Catherine the Great ordered the Admiralty to make its home here. The result was a magnificent fortress-cum-city and port, which became an important commercial port by the mid-18th century. The harbor was used to test submarines, the world's first icebreaker was built here, and it can also proudly claim to be the place where the first radio receiver was built by A. S. Popov in 1895. The pavilion where he worked with Rybkin still stands and can be visited. The city was under siege during the Second World War, and thousands perished; despite this, the city and its citizens played a huge role in the liberation of Leningrad.

Kronstadt is in the district of St. Petersburg, and its stunning St. Nicholas Maritime Cathedral, erected in 1903–13 and initially built as a monument to perished seamen, became a museum in 1980. Seven exhibition halls contain displays about the history of the Kronstadt fortress, the role of the Soviet Navy in the city, Kronstadt during the Second World War, and the city today. Maritime paintings, a substantial number of ship models, parts of ships, minelayers, submarines, and a collection of ancient arms are among the more than 2,500 items on display.

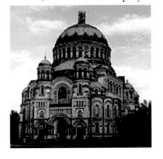

*St. Nicholas
Maritime
Cathedral*

**91**

# The Road of Life
## Дорога Жизни
## Doroga Zhizni

**40**

**Address:** Osinovets Settlement, Vsevolozhskii Region, Leningrad District 188675

**Tel:** 270-69466

**Website:** www.museum.navy.ru

**Open:** 11 A.M.–5:15 P.M., Wednesday to Sunday; closed the last Thursday of every month

**Directions:** Train from Finlandskii Station (metro: Ploshchad' Lenina) to Ladozhskoe Ozero, which is a quarter-mile (600 m) from the museum

Lake Ladoga, the source of the Neva, was the city's lifeline during the siege of Leningrad. In the winter it was possible to ferry much-needed supplies of food and ammunition to the city across the icebound lake. During the warmer months, fuel and communication lines were hidden at the bottom of the lake. This branch of the museum was founded in 1972 and is situated in a one-story building on the banks of the lake. Through photographs, banners, documents, models of ships, weapons and airplanes, river tugs, and motorcars (displayed in the open-air exhibition areas), the museum's exhibits tell of the horrors that faced the Ladoga veterans, as well as their heroism and courage.

*Memorial ensemble 'The Broken Ring', marking the spot where they began to cross the ice*

# Also well worth a visit are . . .

### Apartment-Museum of A. A. Blok
Музей-квартира А. А. Блока
**Muzei-kvartira A. A. Bloka**
A literary and memorial museum dedicated to
the great Symbolist poet
57 Ulitsa Dekabristov, St. Petersburg 190121
Tel: 113-8633 / 113-8631
www.museum.ru/M138

### Apartment-Museum of F. I. Shaliapin
Музей-квартира Ф. И. Шаляпина
**Muzei-kvartira F. I. Shaliapina**
Exhibits illustrate the artistic and personal life of
this talented musician
2b Ulitsa Graftio, St. Petersburg 197022
Tel: 234-1056  www.museum.ru/M162

### Church of the Savior on the Blood
Церковь "Спас на Крови"
**Tserkov' "Spas na Krovi"**
A magnificent symbol of Byzantine architecture
with mosaic interiors
Naberezhnaia Kanala Griboedova 2,
  St. Petersburg 191011
Tel: 314-40-53 www.museum.ru/M179

### Galitzine Memorial Library
Мемориальная Библиотека им Князя.
Галицына
**Memorial'naia Biblioteka im. Kniazia Galitsina**
Anglo-Russian library with a range of cultural
events
46 Naberezhnaia reki Fontanki,
  St. Petersburg 191025
Tel: 311-1333 www.galitzinelibrary.ru

### Gatchina
Гатчина
Grand palace of Paul I and the first landscaped
park in Russia
1 Ekaterinverderskii Prospect, Gatchina,
  Leningradskaia Oblast' 188350
Tel:  271-21509 / 271-23509
www.museum.ru/M242

### Menshikov Palace  Дворец Меншикова
**Dvorets Menshikova**
Palace of Aleksandr Menshikov; first stone
building in the city
15 Universitetskaia Naberezhnaia,
  St. Petersburg 199034
Tel: 213-1112  www.museum.ru/M178

### Mining Museum of the St. Petersburg Mining Institute
Горный музей Санкт Петербургского
Горного Института
**Gornii muzei Sankt Peterburgskogo Gornogo
Instituta**
History of mining with mineralogical and
geological displays
2 line 21, Vasilievskii Ostrov',
  St Petersburg 199026
Tel: 327-8429  www.gorny-ins.ru/museum

### Museum of Decorative-Applied Arts
Музей декоративно-прикладного искусства
**Muzei dekorativno-prikladnogo iskusstva**
A rich and varied collection of applied art,
formerly the property of Baron Stieglitz
13 Solianoi Pereulok, St. Petersburg 191028
Tel:  273-3258 / 273-3804 / 273-5903
www.museum.ru/M181

**93**

## Museum of Russian Political History
Музей Политической Истории России
**Muzei Politicheskoi Istorii Rossii**
Dedicated to the development of revolutionary
movements in Russia
4 Ulitsa Kuibisheva, St. Petersburg 197046
Tel: 233-7266 / 233-7048 / 233-7052
www.museum.ru/Museum/polit_hist/

## Pavlovsk Павловск
Splendid park and palace formerly owned by
Paul I and his wife
20 Ulitsa Revoliutsii, Pavlovsk,
  Leningradskaia Oblast' 196621
Tel: 470-6536 www.pavlovsk.org

## Peterhof Петергоф
Stunning palace and gardens with a superb
collection of fountains
Petrodvorets, 2 Ulitsa Razvodnaia,
St. Petersburg 198903
Tel: 427-9223 / 420-0073 www.peterhof.org

## Sigmund Freud Museum of Dreams
Музей сновидений Зигмунда Фрейда
**Muzei snovidenii Zigmunda Freida**
Exhibitions on psychoanalysis and dream theory
18a Bolshoi Prospect, St. Petersburg 197198
Tel:  235-2857 / 235-2929
www.museum.ru/M2749

## St. Isaac's Cathedral Исаакиевский собор
**Isaakievskii sobor**
The huge cathedral in the heart of the city,
with awe-inspiring interiors
1 Isaakievskaia Ploschad', St. Petersburg 190000
Tel: 315-9732 www.museum.ru/M116

## State Hermitage Museum
Государственный музей Эрмитажа
**Gosudarstvennii muzei Ermitazha**
One of the oldest, largest, and best-known muse-
ums in the world, with 13 miles of galleries housed
in three connected palaces, The Winter Palace and
the Small and Large Hermitages
Dvortsovaia Naberezhnaia 34,
  St. Petersburg 191186
Tel: 311-3601 / 110-9604 / 110-9601
www.hermitagemuseum.org

## State Russian Museum
Государственный Русский Музей
**Gosudarstvennii Russkii Muzei**
Breathtaking collections of Russian art in the
Mikhailovskii Palace, Stroganov Palace, Marble
Palace, and Mikhailovskii Castle
Ulitsa Inzhenernaia 2, St. Petersburg 191011
Tel: 219-1615 / 314-448
www.rusmuseum.ru

## Summer Garden and Summer Palace-Museum of Peter I
Летный сад и Летный дворец-музей Петра 1
**Letnii sad i Letnii dvotets-muzei Petra I**
Collection of western European sculpture and
palace of Paul I
Letnii Sad, 2 Nabererezhnaia Kutuzova,
  St. Petersburg 191041
Tel: 312-7715 / 314-0374
www.museum.ru/M126

# Photographic Credits

The publisher and author wish to thank the following for their kind permission to reproduce the images which appear on the pages noted. Every effort has been made to trace the copyright of all sources and the publishers will be happy to readdress any errors or omissions in future editions.

Sergei Pogodin: pages 17, 20, 21, 35, 38, 40, 47, 48, 52, 62, 63, 65, 72, 73, 75, 76, 77, 79, 83; Eugene Soukharnikov p34; State Russian Museum, St Petersburg, Copyright © page 61 and 66; Tretiakov Gallery, Moscow Copyright © page 67; Wandering Camera (www.enlight.ru/camera) page 71; C.Giangrande cover and page 88; N. Karmazin page 90

Other pictures provided by kind permission of the following museums: Central Naval Museum; Komarov Botanical Museum and Gardens; Historical Artillery Museum; State History Museum; Peter the Great's Log Cabin; Academy of Arts; Peter the Great Museum of Anthropology and Ethnography (Kunstkammer); D. I. Mendeleev Apartment-Museum and Archives; Zoological Museum; History of Religion Museum; All-Russian Museum of A. S. Pushkin; Museum of Circus Art; National Library Museum; Russian Ethnographic Museum; Museum of the Arctic and Antarctic; V. V. Nabokov Museum, State Hermitage Museum and Tsarskoe Selo.

The Russian Association of Travel Agencies for images from the publication *St Petersburg Views*.

# Acknowledgments

I am profoundly grateful to Anna Hart, not only for her outstanding knowledge of Russian, which she put to good use on this book, but also for her research skills, the demands of traveling to St. Petersburg, and her unflagging support. Thanks also to Stephane Burkhard-Sommer, who worked on the formative stages of the book, gathering images and translating material.

The following people were particularly helpful, providing information and images: Irina Aleksandrovna, Museum of the Blockade and Defense of Leningrad; Victor Boyarski, Museum of the Arctic and Antarctic; Irina Ievstigneeva, State Theatrical and Musical Museum; Alexander Kobak, Open Institute and Soros Foundation; Maria Larionova, Museum of the History of Religion; Tatiana Ponomaryova, Nabokov Museum; and Vladimir Timofeev and the employees of the Urban Sculpture Museum.

Sergei Pogodin deserves special thanks for assisting Anna with her museum visits and for his splendid photographs, many of which grace these pages.

A number of friends and colleagues offered advice and were generous with their time, including, Colin Amery and Will Black at the World Monuments Fund in Britain; Susan Causey, Program Officer, Russia, Prince of Wales International Business Leaders Forum; Stephen Dalziel; Errol Fuller; Inna Grigoryeva; Leslee Holderness; and Richard Warner.

I was delighted that John Julius Norwich agreed to write the foreword, as there is no better person than he to endorse the cultural wonders of travel.

At Bunker Hill Publishing, I'd like to thank Ib Bellew and Carole Kitchel, who were enormously supportive, aided by the brilliant work of the designer, Louise Millar. Myles Webb deserves thanks for his scanning skills.

I am indebted to Larry Sullivan, Chairman of CSB Limited, who because of his passion for St. Petersburg generously sponsored the book.

Nobody has done more to bring this work to fruition than those named on the dedication page, my husband Paul and our sons, Chris and Alex, who have endured my many late nights in the office and absences on weekends.

## Sources Consulted and A Guide to Further Reading

Albedil, Margarita, *Saint Petersburg: The Northern Capital of Russia* (St. Petersburg: Alfa-Colour Art Publishers, 2001).

Figes, Orlando. *Natasha's Dance: A Cultural History of Russia* (London: Penguin, 2002).

Galitzine, Katya, *St. Petersburg: The Hidden Interiors* (London: Hazar Publishing, 1999).

Hughes, Lindsey, *Peter the Great, a Biography* (New Haven: Yale University Press, 2002).

Kanaewa, L., *Zarskoje Selo: The Summer Residence of the Russian Czars near Saint Petersburg* (Pushkin: The State Art and Architecture Museum, Park, and Palace Ensemble ).

Margolis, A., *The Museums of St. Petersburg: A Short Guide* (St. Petersburg: EGO Publishers, Institute PRO ARTE, 2000).

*Rossica—International Review of Russian Culture* (London: http://www.users.globalnet.co.uk/ ˜chegeo/rossica.htm; Tel: 00 44 20 7937 5001).

Service, Robert, *Lenin: A Biography* (London: Macmillan, 2000).

Shvidkovsky, Dmitri, *St. Petersburg: Architecture of the Tsars* (New York: Abbeville Press, 1996).

## Useful Websites

The official websites of St. Petersburg: http://eng.gov.spb.ru. & www.spb.ru

The International Association of Libraries and Museums of the Performing Arts: www.theatrelibrary.org/sibmas/sibmas.html

World Monuments Fund, New York: www.worldmonuments.org

World Monuments Fund in Britain has special responsibility for projects in Russia: www.wmf.org.uk

Established by the Union of Creative Museum Workers of St Petersburg and the Leningrad Region and St Petersburg Fund of ICOM, this site lists museums in St. Petersburg: http://eng.allmuseums.spb.ru

Russian Museums Online: www.museum.ru

The Project Russian Art 1860–1940 Information Database: www.art-russia.org

Libraries Hall is a directory of libraries of Russia and the former USSR: www.andrigal.com

Cultivate Interactive is an online web magazine funded by the European Commission's Digital Heritage and Cultural Content (DIGICULT) program: www.cultivate-int.org

Official Site of the Russian National Tourist Office: www.geographia.com/russia/

The St. Petersburg Times: St. Petersburg City Guide: http://cityguide.sptimesrussia.com

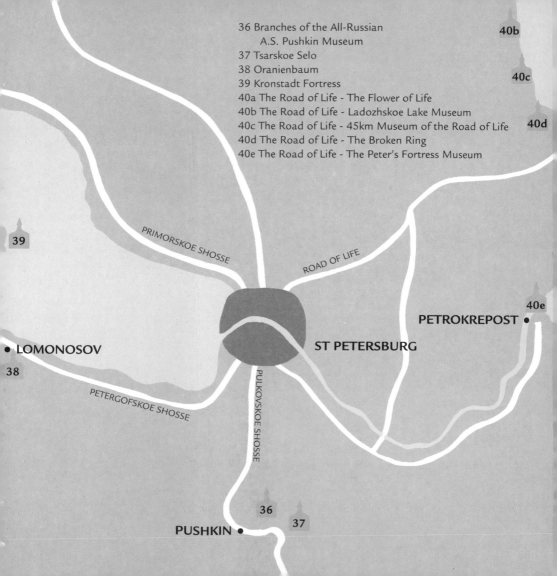

36 Branches of the All-Russian
A.S. Pushkin Museum
37 Tsarskoe Selo
38 Oranienbaum
39 Kronstadt Fortress
40a The Road of Life - The Flower of Life
40b The Road of Life - Ladozhskoe Lake Museum
40c The Road of Life - 45km Museum of the Road of Life
40d The Road of Life - The Broken Ring
40e The Road of Life - The Peter's Fortress Museum

40b

40c

40d

PRIMORSKOE SHOSSE

ROAD OF LIFE

39

40e

LOMONOSOV

ST PETERSBURG

PETROKREPOST

38

PETERGOFSKOE SHOSSE

PULKOVSKOE SHOSSE

36

37

PUSHKIN